Timeless Love

A guide to healing grief and learning to live again

Timeless Love

A guide to healing grief and learning to live again

Patricia L. Bell

Ancient Wisdom Publishing
a division of Nixon-Carre Ltd., Toronto, ON

Copyright © 2010 by Patricia Bell

Library and Archives Canada Cataloguing in Publication

Bell, Patricia L., 1949-
Timeless love : a guide to healing grief and learning to live again / Patricia L. Bell.

ISBN 978-0-9783939-9-1

1. Grief--Religious aspects. 2. Bereavement--Religious aspects. 3. Spiritual healing. I. Title.

BL65.B47B44 2010   204'.42   C2010-900689-5

Published by:
Ancient Wisdom Publishing
A division of Nixon-Carre Ltd.
P.O. Box 92533, Carlton RPO
Toronto, Ontario, M5A 4N9

www.learnancientwisdom.com
www.nixon-carre.com

Distributed by Ingram 1-800-937-8000
www.ingrambook.com

Disclaimer:
Nixon-Carre Ltd. does not participate in, endorse, or take any responsibility for any private business transactions between the author and the public.

This book is sold with the understanding that the publishers are not engaged in rendering legal, medical or other professional advice. If medical or other expert assistance is required, the services of a competent professional should be sought. The information contained herein represents the experiences and opinions of the author, but neither the author or the publisher is responsible for the results of any action taken on the basis of information in this work, nor for any errors or omissions.

Printed and bound in the USA

Contents

This book was written for

Bailey, Alexandria, Matteo, Sandra, James and Michael Bell

Dedicated to

Leonard Chetkin

Special thanks to

Taryn Floodman

My guardian angel, goddaughter,
and godmother to this book.
She has been my balance throughout
this project, and a light of inspiration.

Foreword

Perhaps the greatest mystery for most human beings is the mystery of death. Where do we go when we die? Do we go anywhere, or is it just the end of life? And then there's the mystery surrounding the many circumstances of death itself. Why do some die in the prime of their life? Why does a child die before he or she has had a chance to live? Why do some survive a horrible automobile accident and others die trying to swallow a piece of steak? Why . . . why . . . why? So many questions. Does God allow the good to die young? Does God choose who is to live and who is to survive? Does love survive death? Is there a plan here, or is it all just the luck of the draw?

In Timeless Love, Patricia Bell gives us all some answers. When someone close to us passes on, there is inevitable pain. And the questions always come. If we could have a better understanding of death, and the life beyond death, it would literally shift our entire perspective of life. It would certainly comfort us to know that our loved one is still living, if in another dimension, but still alive in spirit if not in body.

Having gone through her own grief in losing a beloved husband when she was only 22, Patricia Bell knew firsthand what grief was like. She came through a searing, gut-wrenching grief that almost destroyed her. And she went on to learn how to teach others to deal with death, with grief, and with doubt. Ms. Bell is a gifted medium and psychic who learned how to overcome her loss, and to find happiness again.

And here in this wonderful book, she shares that knowledge with all of us. She learned that death is not the end-it's the beginning. She learned how to heal, and how to teach us how to heal as well. No one who has ever experienced a loss will ever forget Timeless Love.

Robert S. Friedman,
co-author of ***Milton's Secret***
with Ekhart Tolle

Author's Preface

Dear Reader,

Much has been written about the psychological effects of coping with loss. Though many theorists have designed stages and categories for grief that help us to understand the powerful emotions associated with it, little has been written about the spiritual crisis that occurs during grief or spiritual healing. I decided to write this book to share what I have experienced in my own healing journey and what I practice in my work as a Spiritualist Minister and Registered Medium: The healing of grief requires more than psychological support. It requires using the power of love to create a new life.

No one can really understand what grief is like until we experience the death of someone we dearly love. It is an event that transforms each of us in body, mind, and soul. Although being torn from the most significant relationships in our lives is definitely the time when personal growth is least on our minds, the death of a loved one is the event that creates the greatest opportunity for growth. It is the event that reminds us of our true purpose - to understand the true meaning of compassion and love.

I had no idea how much my life would change when my husband, Gaetano, died. His death started me on a search to find where his love had gone - the love that I cherished every day of our lives together. It was the beginning of a journey that changed my life forever. During the ten years that followed, I had an unquenchable thirst for knowledge of Spirit. I discovered that spirituality went far beyond going to church. In my quest, I realized that healing and communicating beyond death is possible for each of us because: "Love is timeless and it changes us forever".

For the past 35 years, I have traveled all over the world sharing Divine gifts that I call "gifts from Spirit." I lead workshops on healing and spiritual communication all across the United States, as well as in many cultures that are very different from my own. One of the many things that I have discovered is no matter how different we appear on the surface, grief is universal and the yearning for spiritual healing is common to everyone.

Spiritual healing is as old as humanity and is available to all of us. There is nothing unusual or odd about our spiritual needs. Taking care of these needs is as essential to our lives as the air we breathe, and the food we eat.

As you work through the same meditations that I use in my workshops, you will be able to release the pain that blocks the joy that you are meant to have. You will discover how to align your body, emotions and soul through Spirit and receive a new purpose in your life through these powerful exercises. You will step forward into your future knowing that love and healing are yours for the asking.

This book looks at the spiritual origins and nature of common grief responses, interprets them from a spiritual point of view, and provides strategies for spiritual recovery from these crises. There are many healing messages and meditations to help you as you move through your personal healing journey.

Whether you are beginning your journey soon after the death of a loved one, or are well on the healing path, this book will teach you how to use the power of Divine Love to create a new life filled with happiness.

Don't be afraid to heal. The Divine Love that flows from Spirit is always focused on healing, serving, and improving the quality of your life.

Come; prepare to experience healing. Allow the gentle language of Spirit to flow through you. Embrace the journey that is uniquely yours, and receive the healing treasures of Spirit.

With deep and abiding love,
Patricia Bell
Lily Dale, NY
September 2009

A Love Story

My opportunity for spiritual growth occurred on January 6, 1972, with the death of my beloved husband, Gaetano. On that day, I stepped onto the path of a spiritual journey that not only healed me, but gave me the beautiful gift of communicating with loved ones who have returned to their perfect spiritual state. I had no idea how much my life would change. It was a journey that began in grief and suffering, from which I thought I could never be released.

I was a young girl working in my father's restaurant on the beach in Florida when one day a handsome, fit man walked in. He was just back from service in the navy, and had moved to Florida to begin a new life. From the moment we saw each other there was a powerful attraction. In that moment, all I knew was that I wanted to be with him. We married soon after my 19th birthday, settled into our new family life together, started having babies and couldn't be happier.

Then on Jan 6, 1972 he boarded a train from New York's Penn Station headed back to Florida, returning from a trip to visit his mother. On the train he had a massive heart attack. He was only 27 years old. I was 22 and left a widow with two children.

When Gaetano died, it seemed the wonderful love that once flowed between us died with him. In grief, I was left with nothing but pain to fill the hollow space where our love used to be. No matter how many times I turned things over and over in my mind, the loss of my precious husband, the father of our two beautiful children, left nagging questions that would not go away.

My feeling that love died with Gaetano haunted me. I felt like I had somehow been deceived about the nature of love, and I simply could not bear the consequences of such a revelation. If it was true that when the physical body goes then the love goes with it, love could not exist beyond space and time. Meaningfulness and purposefulness in all things were just an illusion - nothing seemed real but my pain.

At first, I turned to the religious person most

familiar, Father Gunter, the Catholic priest who had married us. He was gentle, and a very devout man. Six hours passed while he consoled me as I wept and wailed about Gaetano's death. He comforted me with words of tenderness, and acknowledged my pain as a natural response to loss. Though his sympathy and encouragement was genuine, I was inconsolable. I droned on with questions that he could not answer to my satisfaction.

"Why?" I pleaded as I begged him for answers.

None came.

The Priest reminded me that I was very young and that my future lay before me. However, in the midst of grief, time no longer mattered to me. I felt suspended outside of it, and could no longer see ahead. All of my plans, my future, were gone in an instant.

The more Father Gunter attempted to pull me out of my despair, the more I felt removed from the world around me. When he tried to get me to focus on the needs of my children, I could only focus on the fact that they were without their loving father, and we would never hear from him again. I was devastated.

Death, to me, was the end, beyond which there was nothing but treacherous questions.

"How could God do this to us?" I ranted until I was exhausted.

Weary and confused, I left this dear, sweet priest after this marathon of grieving, with no answers. I am certain, given his experience and wisdom, that he could see the tremendous challenges that faced me. He knew what I did not yet know, about the nature of Divine Love and he trusted in God's plan to get me through this crisis. I, on the other hand, only wanted answers.

I did not think about healing. I could not. I only thought that there had to be answers that would set everything right. I thought if I could talk to the right person, they could give me answers. I was determined. I was going to get the answers I was seeking even if it took going to every church in town.

The next day, I sat on the steps of another church, a huge and beautifully old one, and wept. Somehow I knew the solace I was seeking could only come from God, but I did not know how or where to find God. I thought if I only knew why Gaetano was taken away from me, I could bear the unbearable. If I could only know what happens to love when we die, where it goes and why, I could somehow awaken from this nightmare.

When I tried to open the doors to the church, they were locked. At that moment something changed inside of me. My faith and trust were shattered. Those huge heavy doors kept me from entering the place where I thought I would find answers. Although I did not think it possible, it drove me deeper into the pain of my broken heart.

With each step that I took as I walked away, the love that I had for Gaetano fell from my heart like petals from a dying flower. Once fresh and beautiful in the light of his love, it now withered and died in the darkness of my grief. The springtime of my life had suddenly turned into the dead of winter. I was cold and numb from pain. The bleakness of fear and sadness became the only emotional weather I knew. I had no idea whether spring would ever come again.

During the months that followed, I was plagued with many questions that went unanswered. Still, at the end of each day, the most haunting question remained: "Where does love go when people die?" If God always loves me, there has to be a way that those people that are with God could love me too.

I struggled with my thoughts day and night until I became exhausted. "It's real. I know it's real. I felt it. It happened to me 'out of the blue.' I gave myself up to it. I grew in it. I gave it. I received it. It was supposed to go on forever!"

I was obsessed with finding where love goes when people die. I refused to accept that the pure and wonderful love I shared with Gaetano every day of our lives could have vanished, as though it never existed!

I knew nothing of the intimate ways of Spirit and had no concept of a healing journey. I just kept living with no particular direction in mind, unable to see that Spirit was leading me. No doubt, the prayers of Father Gunter were stepping-stones on the path before me, and Spirit was guiding me through the many changes.

For the ten years that followed, I had an unquenchable thirst for knowledge about our spiritual existence. I explored psychotherapy, I delved into Western doctrines of Judeo-Christian origins, and I studied many other religions and saw how they all work together as a path to God. I love the combination of Eastern and Western religious traditions that emphasize spiritual development through experience and affiliation instead of simply one or the other.

Along the way, I met many people who came from traditions where the emphasis of life is on experiencing spirituality. These people had done the work of spiritual development and dedicated their lives to helping those of us who seek to be healed. Several of these wonderful teachers became my mentors. They instructed me in practices from the Cabala, Yoga, and Eastern mysticism to deepen my spiritual connection, and allow me to master the practices of meditation and yoga, that are now embraced by the Western world. I also learned to interpret and depend on the many forms of Divine guidance, sometimes in the form of subtle cues, or metaphorical language, and the powerful urges from the spiritual realm.

From the depths of despair, Divine Love healed me. I grew in love and awareness of the Spirit within me. I was healed from the Source of all healing, and at long last knew the deep truth: Love is timeless and transcends death.

Out of suffering came my calling. By the time I was ordained as a Spiritualist Minister in 1986, I was already sharing the many gifts of Spirit by teaching healing practices of meditation, and guiding hundreds in the subtle intricacies of spiritual communication with loved ones who have transcended physical existence.

Each of us has to be led along the healing journey back to the Divine Love that sustains us. When we seek to heal grief, our spiritual ears and eyes are opened. Whenever a heart is deepened through suffering, a great change awaits us, a transformation made possible by the death of a beloved so that we, too, can come home to the eternal place of the soul.

The work of spiritual healing is so much more than belonging to a particular church, or simply believing in the existence of a Higher Power. You must unlock the Divine mysteries of your personal relationship with your Creator.

Just like physical and emotional development, healing requires your cooperation and active involvement in the spiritual process.

It may be difficult to believe when you are suffering, but grief can be healed, and your life can be restored. Step onto the path of your spiritual journey and keep walking, through the pain into the compassionate arms of your Spiritual-Self, that spark of God within you.

Healing Message

Love is never lost, even in death

Use this message to regain your own personal understanding, strength, and perception on your healing journey.

Say it even if it feels uncomfortable at first. It will help you to go into another state, free of the sorrow and pain in order to connect with the higher levels of yourself.

When we love anything in life, we share a part of ourselves. In this healing message we know that our love goes on.

Love is never lost, even in death.

Invite Spirit into your life to create the balance that you need. Take a few moments and let this healing message sink in. Read it slowly, several times until you begin to speak the words out loud:

Love is never lost, even in death.

Make these words your words. Listen to them as you speak. Close your eyes and let the healing message wash over you. Feel it move through you. Give yourself special permission to believe the words:

"Love is never lost, even in death."

When you can feel the love alive and vital, let your pain go. Begin to feel the love holding you, rocking you, accept its gift of new hope for the next moment.

A Spiritual Emergency

In the midst of your grief, it may be difficult for you to believe that hope and joy will ever return to your life. I understand the ache and terror that seems unrelenting. The constant chatter of unanswered questions is tormenting.

Just when you think you can get through a day, the confusion, helplessness, and agony take you by surprise, again. Overwhelmed, you wonder whether you will ever be able to function as you once did. It feels like the past has a hold on you and will not let you get on with your life. When you are stuck in grief, you cannot even grasp the day.

However, love is never lost, even in death. Be gentle and patient with yourself. The power of the love that you shared can be used to create a new life filled with hope and joy.

When someone you love dies the only emotions you recognize are pain and despair. Even after the initial shock fades and the numbness passes, you are still filled with soul-wrenching thoughts:

"Why can't I let go?"

"Why do I feel as if my loved one still lives inside my heart and my mind?"

"Why does my beloved seem to be around me all the time?"

"Why do I still act as if his or her feelings and needs direct everything I think and do - everything I wish for, everything I dream?"

We try to save ourselves from these plaguing questions. We try to find relief in the well-meaning words of friends and family. You may try to hide in your home or bury yourself in work. In grief we look for the tiniest, temporary solace and keep moving, feeling alone, empty, and exhausted.

Sometimes we try to reason with grief by looking for some way to justify the death of a beloved, hoping for a brief moment of comfort or relief.

We have all said the words:

"He's in a better place."

"At least she's not in pain anymore."

"Be thankful you had him in your life for as long as you did."

"We must put our trust in God and know that this, too, is part of His Divine Plan."

Although this mental reasoning can provide some temporary relief, it does little to soothe the soul. In the quietest moments a broken heart continues to overflow with pain. The emptiness rises like a tide and threatens to drown us. Some of us may even sink downward into what feels like an abyss of anger and futility, and experience panic as we search for a way out of the solitary darkness. Our thoughts reinforce our feelings of helplessness:

"Where do I go now?"

"How do I create a new life?"

"How can I ever find happiness again without my partner, soul-mate, best friend, child, that I loved beyond words?"

"Where is this strange emptiness taking me?"

Though the answers may never come, the questions will become less important as you enter healing, and your new life unfolds. As we learn about the nature of grief, we can overcome it.

The emotional ups and downs create mental exhaustion and erode our physical health. Some people need to be reminded to eat, drink, and get out of the house to go for a walk or do minimal exercise to avoid serious illness. Even after we regain physical strength and an emotional foothold, grief creates a spiritual emergency by blocking the way to Divine Love.

Grief feels like forever. Grief lies and tells you, "Love is lost." For those who are stuck in grief, this is the lie that you begin to believe. In addition to this lie that makes us cling to the past, the trust and faith that sustain us are often shattered. The pain of grief makes healing seem impossible.

What is worse, grief barricades the heart and leaves you unable to feel the love that still abounds. This is the spiritual emergency that goes along with the physical weakness and emotional devastation of losing a loved one through death. When grief cuts us off from the healing power of Divine Love, it also robs us of the deep abiding love that speaks to us and heals us. It blocks our connection to Spirit.

Use the exercises in this book to attune your heart to awareness of Spirit guiding you. When you let Spirit carry you, you begin to hear the subtle communication that is constant between our physical and spiritual realities. Spirit will tear down the barricade to the heart and dispel the lies.

The gentle meditations in this book will help the power of Spirit to be present in your life, and fill you with Divine Love. Divine Love restores trust, rebuilds faith, and allows you to discover the beauty of the connection between body, mind, and soul through which Spirit flows. When you accept the healing power of Divine Love and discover the secrets that you were meant to understand in the death transformation, you are freed from devastating grief.

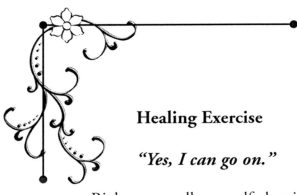

Healing Exercise

"Yes, I can go on."

Right now, tell yourself that it is possible for you to be restored and renewed. Healing is possible. Remind yourself of the healing message:

"Love is never lost, even in death."

When we say things out loud, we are able to hear the words in a different way. Speaking positive messages makes the noise in your mind decrease as you actually listen to the words you speak. Rather than have your power absorbed by the pain in your mind, you can begin to give your mind healthful instructions to follow. This is done in the form of affirmations.

These simple, yet powerful, affirmations open up a door of communication with Spirit. They tell your subconscious mind that you are ready and willing to heal. Speak them aloud to yourself. Print them on pieces of paper and place them wherever you are likely to see them throughout the day and night. They have proven to boost hope and energy in healing work. Say them as often as you feel the need:

"Yes, I can go on because healing grief is possible."

"Yes, I want to go on because Spirit will restore my life."

"Yes, I will go on because Divine Love is mine for the asking."

Oh, Time you merciless beast.

You laugh aloud at us mere mortals
that acknowledge your presence.

Be gone with you Time,
and take thy brother Reality with you,
and in that fleeting moment
my love shall return to me
and I say have no need of either of you.

Patricia L. Bell

The Spiritual Connection

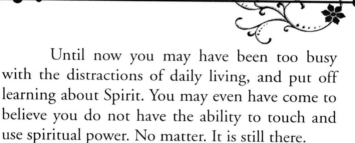

Until now you may have been too busy with the distractions of daily living, and put off learning about Spirit. You may even have come to believe you do not have the ability to touch and use spiritual power. No matter. It is still there.

The ability to connect to your inner spiritual power remains with you for all time. Even though you may not have realized it, Spirit has guided you throughout your entire life. But, just like a muscle that grows weak from lack of use, your connection to Spirit has to be exercised if it is to grow strong and vital.

People often worry about whether they need to belong to a particular church, believe a certain thing, or have the right upbringing to connect to Spirit. However, no particular religion or philosophy has a corner on the truth. Each has something to offer. While we all benefit from the support of a spiritual community, we each need to find our own spiritual path. The Bible, the Torah, the Koran, the I Ching, Baghivadgita, Upanishads, Urantia, and thousands of other Divinely inspired scriptures throughout human history reveal the same simple message: "Seek and ye shall find."

We are all part of the divine oneness that is. By stepping out on our own spiritual journey, we are able to create a pathway for all there is to be one with us. If we are all one, God is within the divine perception within each individual. Even if you are an atheist or connected to a certain spiritual community, your understanding of God throughout your life has been represented by the energy inside of you that connects you to what is beyond. Spiritually, this is Divine Love.

I respect your choice of whatever concept of God is comfortable for you, and I encourage you to substitute the words that apply to that concept as you read. No matter what word or image you prefer to use, it is the same Divine Love that we all seek for wholeness and healing.

We all recognize that there is some sort of powerful presence within us-a source of healing, motivation, and courage, usually called the soul. It is here that we come in contact with a deep knowledge that goes beyond words. You can become aware of the movement of Spirit within you. Its power nourishes us, inspires us, and bathes us in love. You can experience for yourself that love never dies. Everyone is connected to Spirit. That spark of the Creator is your soul within you. Spirit is the force that gives you life, energy, and power. It is the spark of the Divine and the source of goodness and god-ness.

In the same way that imagination and emotions exist on internal levels and are not so obvious, Spirit within you moves through your inner world. You intuitively know the Spirit within you. You recognize the energy and move toward it. Spirit reaches from its home in the soul to your mind and body, and will do whatever needs to be done to help you through this challenging time. You are given all the love and support you need to handle your challenges. In truth, there is not a single moment in your life when your connection to Divine Love has failed. It is simply that you have forgotten you have it.

Everything you need to know to help you heal the pain of loss and understand the nature and mystery of Divine Love is hidden within the spiritual part of your being. But before you can reach into yourself for answers, you must understand that all your challenges in this life are for the enrichment of your understanding of love and compassion. You will never encounter more than you are capable of handling.

Everything that you need to fully appreciate a joyful life is right here within you.

Our awareness exists on many levels of the body, the mind, and soul. The physical world is only one part of our lives. Most people accept the idea that the mind, body, and soul are all connected. It means that we are so much more than how we look, think, or act. You may not be aware that throughout your entire life you have the ability to connect to other levels of awareness in body, mind, and soul. You are truly connected in mind, body, and soul to Divine Love.

The answers to all our questions lie buried deeply in our hearts and await the quickening that comes with Spirit to unlock them. But before you approach your heart that is barricaded with disappointment, anger, fear, and despair you must be ready to use the knowledge, be willing to give your pain away and replace it with healing. Forsake the language of pain, and learn the language of the heart, the language of the Spirit.

Allow the power of Divine Love to heal you and restore your life.

As a Spiritualist minister, one of the major principles is the ongoing communication with life. The way we are able to communicate with someone beyond their "death" is because a person's energy remains timeless. Everything and everyone is energy, and energy continually transforms. This is the life cycle.

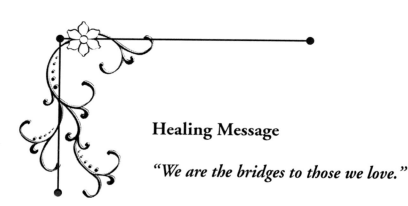

Healing Message

"We are the bridges to those we love."

Although God's plan is so much bigger than we are, it depends upon us. The beauty of creation depends on us to see and enjoy it. Joy depends on us to share it and use its power, to renew our lives. Hope is a gift from Spirit to remind us of our spiritual origins and know that a new day is coming. When we see beauty and joy and hope in others, we allow them to see it, too. We are all connected.

The world doesn't want to lose another heart to grief. Share this healing message with someone who depends on you. Think about how beautiful they are. As you speak this message out loud, begin to realize that you are connected to people through love and that the well of love never runs dry.

Let someone know that they are important to you and to the world. Thank them for being creative and courageous in their own life.

Creating Your Sacred Space

4

Nothing occurs without a space and a time in which to happen.

When I am working with people in a workshop or in private consultation, I create an environment where they feel relaxed, comfortable, and open to Spirit within. The workshop space feels protected and energized.

You can create that space for yourself, so that you have your own special place to heal.

Ideally, you should have a physical place somewhere where you can create your own boundaries. This can be as simple as a single chair or a spot in a garden. Do whatever you can to create this physical space for healing and meditation.

Many people think that they can't create a

space for themselves because of their busy lives, but we all need this. How can you expect to talk to Spirit when you're continually busy?

Grief is a strong force that resists letting go. The past has a strong grip on your emotions, but healing grief is an active journey into your future.

It is time to put aside the way things used to be, and begin the healing process. I am not saying that you must forget, or give up all your wonderful memories. Certainly not! However, healing grief is an active process in the here and now. Your spiritual, mental, and physical accomplishments all occur in the active mode. Healing grief is no different. You must get involved with healing to receive the gifts of Spirit. Making a place and time to heal is a part of your active involvement with Spirit.

Creating your sacred space is your message to yourself and to Spirit that you want to reclaim your life. Although it may seem simple, it is a powerful exercise that works on your mind, body, and soul at the same time. It sends a message of your intention to heal. It is another kind of positive affirmation.

The space that you create happens on the inside as well as on the outside, in your mind as well as your environment. Just as you set aside a corner or a room as your place to do this work, your mind makes a space for you to do this on the inside. Your Sacred Space is the place and time for you to be reconnected to Divine Love.

Many people know how to create their own space naturally, but may not realize how important it is until someone points it out to them. Some have a favorite chair and reading lamp, or quiet time behind a locked bedroom or bathroom door where they can be away from the telephone and television. I have some friends whose households are so hectic they actually sit in their parked car for a moment's peace to read or pray. What is really important is not where or when you make your own space, but that you do create this time and place, and regard it with just as much importance as a visit to the doctor or therapist.

If at all possible, make a place right now, where you can simply "be" when you read this book. Create something more than squeezing in a couple of pages of reading while you are waiting in a line, or writing a shopping list. Give yourself some serious time to get involved with Spirit.

A good way to begin to prepare your sacred space and place is to think about what nourishes you. Take a moment and look for things in your environment that promote feelings of relaxation, peace, health, and vitality, and begin to gather them into an area where you can establish some private time.

Each of us has items that are uniquely ours in the sense that they make us feel comfortable. Sometimes these items such as a plant, a candle, favorite scents and textures, special lighting can all be arranged in a small area, a corner or on a table, or even in a bathroom so that you can use them to nurture yourself. Gather whatever you have that helps you to feel quiet and calm and create a sacred space physically and spiritually, externally and internally, and a time to begin this journey.

Making the time and the place to grow in the love that nourishes you assures that you are ready to receive it. Even if it is only for a few minutes each day, it is your sacred space, your special time and place where you can seek soulful refuge. You deserve to heal. You deserve to be joyous. You deserve the gift of this time and space.

The healing journey is a sacred experience that lives so tenderly and completely in the heart that we must protect it until we grow strong and active in our relationship to Spirit.

I encourage you to let your friends and

family know that you are undertaking a personal endeavor to heal. Tell them what you are doing so that they will respect your space and time and not feel ignored or disregarded. There is no need to go into great detail. The changes in you will say more than words ever could.

Living in awareness of Spirit, I have learned that truth and light, real knowledge and happiness is to be found in everyday life - in living every moment. After all, we purposely came to this physical life on earth to enjoy what it has to offer and to learn through love. I have found that one of the best ways to explore our connection to Spirit is through the centuries old practice of meditation.

Meditation prepares us to receive knowledge and healing through our connection to Divine Love. For the first meditation, I have chosen one that increases your brain's energy and helps expand awareness of the spiritual areas. As the mind relaxes, you begin to open abilities that you do not use everyday, and are able to look into spiritual places.

During this first healing meditation, you will visualize the beautiful colors of the spectrum, the colors of the rainbow. This is a simple, beginning exercise. Take time to read through it as you prepare yourself to participate. You can come to this meditation anytime, and return as often as you need.

The perceptions in meditation are unique to the person doing the meditation. So do not pass judgment on yourself, just allow yourself to experience what is happening, whether it is feelings, thoughts, visions, sound, or smell.

Many people think that they are unable to visualize. If you are one of these people try using the word "imagine" instead of "visualize".

Healing Meditation

Releasing the Mind

Go into your sacred space and find a comfortable sitting position. Some people prefer to lie down, but this position makes it difficult to avoid going to sleep. It is not necessary to sit cross legged on the floor unless this is a comfortable position for you. The important thing is to be comfortable.

Close your eyes. Feel your mind begin to leave the business of the day behind.

Drop your shoulders. Feel your body begin to let go of its burden as you notice a comfortable easiness move through you.

Take a deep breath. Exhale. Feel the release.

Begin by imagining the color RED. See it through its entire gradient from pale to deep richness. Slowly exhale. Allow the RED to melt in your brain.

Take another deep breath and visualize the color ORANGE. Again, exhale and feel the color ORANGE throughout your entire brain.

Take another deep breath and visualize YELLOW. As the yellow circulates through your brain, exhale, and sense that the color YELLOW has moved through your entire brain.

Now, with another deep breath, visualize the color GREEN. Allow the GREEN to flow inside your head. Exhale.

Breathe deeply. Fill your head with the color of BLUE SKY. Allow the beautiful SKY BLUE to float through your brain. Exhale, slowly.

Take a deep breath and fill your head with the color PURPLE, the color of irises. Visualize the PURPLE saturating your entire brain. Slowly breathe out the color PURPLE.

With another deep breath, breathe in the color WHITE. Allow the soft white to absorb into your brain.

As you breathe deeply and evenly, visualize a figure "8" as an image pattern. Let the figure "8" move back and forth from right to left. As you visualize the "8" moving backward and forward, imagine a soft cloth massaging your brain.

Take three deep breathes in and out. Begin to visualize electric waves going through the temples of your head from right to left, left to right, back to front, top to bottom.

Breathing deeply and evenly, feel your whole brain refresh and recharge as the soft cloth massages in a figure "8" and the electrical waves go through your head.

Again visualize the colors RED, ORANGE, YELLOW, GREEN, BLUE, PURPLE.

Continue to experience the colors moving in and out of your awareness until you feel drawn to open your eyes.

Exhale and stretch.

To everything there is a season,
And a time to every purpose
under the heaven:
A time to be born, and a time to die.

Ecclesiastes 3:1-2 (KJV)

Discovering Your Spiritual Self

The physical world is only one dimension of our lives. Just as the body needs physical exercise, our soul needs the exercise of loving and growing in that love through all of life's changes. We must allow love to transform us through our connection to Divine Love. Just like a muscle that grows weak from lack of use, our bond to Spirit has to be exercised to grow strong and vital. We do this through the many kinds of love that we are given to explore such as our relationships with family, friends, pets, acquaintances, even strangers, as well as of the beauty in the world around us.

As we understand more about these relationships, we discover more about the spiritual part of our being.

Each time we stop to appreciate the beauty of a red rose, or a purple wild flower, love grows.

Each time we perform an act of kindness to a stranger, love grows and the world becomes a better place. For every hurt feeling and misunderstanding between loved ones that is forgiven or reconciled through the power of love, our connection to Divine Love is strengthened. As we learn about loving, our souls grow brighter, deeper, more beautiful and full. Through our appreciation of beauty we are all brought a little closer to our spiritual origins.

I think of the soul as the place of our deeper existence where our spiritual nature lives, and remembers our connection to God. It is also the spark of the Creator within us, the force that gives life, energy, power, and love, from the Source of all goodness and god-ness. It is where we discover our spiritual-self.

The spiritual-self is not the creation of the mind, or religion, or superstition. It is the part of us that comes from our spiritual origins in the ethereal, and is connected to the presence of Spirit within us. Spirit stands ready to serve us in the same way that a loving parent stands ready to protect and guide a very precious child. You are that child.

You intuitively know the spiritual-self deep within your soul. You recognize it as the true "you" and move toward it in your deepest moments. It reaches from its ethereal home down into your life on earth, to help you, guide you, and grow with you.

Everything you need to know to heal the pain of loss, and understand the mystery of Divine Love, is hidden within the spiritual part of your being. Everything you need in order to fully appreciate a joyful life is right here within you. Divine Love is within, for you to draw on. When you experience the love that flows to you from Spirit, a new awareness guides you. Your life has greater meaning, certainty, and purpose.

People always ask: "How do I know how much spiritual ability I have?"

Maybe they believe that they have never had the ability to touch and use spiritual power. You may feel that way, too. Perhaps the best way for me to answer this question is to guide you into a glimpse of your daily life the way your soul sees it and helps you.

Think about the origin of "gut feelings" and "hunches". Where do they come from? How many times have you depended on them or used them to help you make decisions? How do you recognize them? How do you communicate with them? What is it about them that cause you to act? You may be unaware of many of the times when Spirit has spoken to you this way. The special sense of knowing that happens deep inside is one of the many ways that Spirit guides you, and participates in your daily life.

Truth is, throughout your life, you have experienced many instances of Divine Love and communication with Spirit. You may have suspicions that Spirit intervened to save you during some extraordinary event in your life. You may even have several experiences in which you know, without a doubt, that God guided you. Look through your memories and recall these times. Even the simplest of moments is significant, and can put you in contact with Spirit.

As you begin to think about these things, reflect on the extraordinary way that you can sense the presence of other people nearby, or know when you are being looked at by someone in the car next to you. Think about how you understand and interpret the things that happen around you.

What words do you use to explain events? Do you use words like luck, chance, coincidence and synchronicity? Do you ever say, "Thank God", or feel that something happened in your favor when you could not possibly have influenced a favorable outcome?

Each of us has spiritual ability. It is always

with us - our connection to our ethereal home.

Most of us seek to make contact with God quite naturally, and very frequently. We know there is some grand scheme of things - a Divine plan, of which we are a part. We depend on it by the things we say and do. We trust the sun to rise and set and the moon and stars to light the night. We "fly by the seats of our pants" with a deeper knowing that Spirit is there, within us, ready to pick us up when we fall or fail. There is never a time in our lives when we are without spiritual ability or the connection to Divine Love.

Healing grief is a journey that brings us closer to remembering what we are and where we have been. Every single moment has a new piece of information, a missing part of our life puzzle, a flicker of our Divine existence, and insight into all our spiritual experiences. After a significant loss, a period of transition occurs when we are strongly connected to Spirit and are being transformed. We slowly begin to grasp the changes in our life. When we heal through the power of Divine Love, we also have a new identity and a new relationship with Spirit to help us.

As you begin to appreciate your transformation, you may find that your love for the simplest of things, a child's smile, a leaf on the wind, becomes amplified.

The texture of life seems richer, more sustaining. Even so, you begin to realize that there is a deep sense of familiarity with all of it. Know you are not alone. You are not a stranger in a strange place. You are an integral part of everything. You have discovered your connection to Divine Love that ceaselessly flows into your life and that connection can never be broken. It is there for you to draw upon for all your needs.

As you begin to reach deeply inside for answers, you see that birth and death are part of the Divine plan that begins and ends in the spiritual world, and you are a spiritual being who is here to grow in lessons of the heart.

In a grand and precious cycle of events, we are given many opportunities to embrace life on this earth and grow in our primary purpose-to continually understand love and become closer to Spirit. Your spirit, the soul of your being (your spiritual-self) came to this earthly life by choice from the spiritual world. In other words, your soul did not grow in your mother's womb along with your body. Rather, your spiritual body chose to leave that realm - call it heaven, the Great Void, God/Goddess - and return to learn the lessons of love on earth in your physical form. Mind/Body/Spirit, together, made this transition so you could learn, grow, create, experience, all the gifts of this life and carry new gifts to the next.

What lessons will you learn? What treasures will you take from this life into the next? This beautiful journey is your chance to evolve in your understanding of the meaning of life through the meaning of love, and become aware of your part of the Divine plan.

Before leaving that God-source your spirit made many choices. It chose the problems you needed to face, the paths you needed to walk, and the people you needed to love. Meetings with special people for special reasons, all having to do with helping you to grow in your understanding of the power of Divine Love were planned before their moment in time on this earth. Losses were seen, and the pain of them already known, so that you could move to a new level of loving, drawing ever closer to the Divine Creator. The choice to do the work of healing and growth, however, is yours. Your freedom and free will are unhindered. Using all the events throughout your lifetime to grow in Divine love is entirely up to you.

From the immortal knowledge we know that life and death are a cycle. We all arrive through the womb, and are woven into the fabric of all that we touch, and all that touches us. Too quickly, our senses are overloaded. Time binds us and measures our lives between events and places. We forget the language of Spirit. We struggle to hear the gentle sounds, feelings, and sights from our spiritual home. Soon, we forget that we are spiritual beings with an extraordinary purpose.

In the "here and now", when someone you love dies, healing begins as you strive to remember the spiritual reason he or she was in your life. We each begin by reconnecting to our spiritual-self and asking for answers. For a moment, think about all the people in your life. Focus on someone and begin to ask these questions:

"Why did I plan to be involved with this person?"

"What am I to learn?"

"What kind of love am I experiencing?"

"What will I take forth into my own spirit?"

"Did I give or receive something unique to, or from this person?"

By reaching into your spiritual-self for answers, you can begin to learn who you really are right now, in this moment. You can know completeness and fulfillment, and grow in the love that never dies. As you grow in understanding of the relationships in the course of your life, no matter how brief or how long, your awareness of the spirit within you begins to deepen.

When our spirit moved from the spiritual to the earthly world, we buried these answers deep within our soul. To heal grief, we must be courageous and be willing to admit that it is all right for us to have a new life without the person who died-even if we still have unfinished business with them, negative feelings about them, or guilt over some incident, even their death.

The first step is to learn who we really are right now. Asking your spiritual-self for deeper knowledge means inviting Divine Spirit to lead the way in your excavation of the soul's long forgotten treasures. I fully believe that everyone can do this throughout our entire life on earth, but since most of us are not aware that we can, we don't.

It is no secret that everyone has his or her own level of physical ability. We certainly are not all NFL quarterbacks, Olympic swimmers, or PGA golfers. We each have our own mental abilities, too. Some people are good with numbers, others with words. Spiritual abilities work the same way. We each have our own degree of ability for tapping into them - just like we each have our own path to walk. What we share, however, is the Source, and no matter where you are on your healing journey, meditation can help you connect to the power of Divine Love and heal your grief.

While no one can promise that every meditation or exercise will produce an exact result, I can promise that the quality of your life will improve if you use the exercises in this book repeatedly. People progress at different paces. Your pace is unique to you. Become aware of the little things in your life. You may find that your sense of humor is stronger at certain times, or your intuition more keen, or your thoughts clearer at some times than others. The deep inner workings of healing do not always come into the mind, but often is revealed in subtle changes in your thoughts and feelings that give you an "Ah Ha!" experience.

Be patient. Divine Love is always there for you, even though you may not always be able to feel it immediately. It takes time to break the hold of grief. Respect it and refocus your mind on healing.

Healing Message

The Rainbow After the Storm

Just as the rainbow promises a new day, when I visualize its beautiful colors in meditation I, too, am brought into a new day, to heal after the storm.

Before we move into a new understanding of the kinds of relationships that we have throughout our lives, and begin to understand each particular kind of loss with the death of a beloved, take this healing message to heart, let it strengthen you and give you courage for a new day.

Return to your sacred space and reflect on this healing message. Repeat the first meditation that energized your brain and released your mind. Know that you can return to it anytime you need to re-energize and open up those places that you do not use everyday.

Healing Exercise

Your Spiritual Journal

There is a kind of magic that happens when we write things down. The simple act of recording our experiences helps us to integrate them into our body, mind, and soul. Writing our thoughts and feelings, and describing inner awakenings gives us a way of working with our inner lives in the here and now of the external world.

Keeping a Spiritual Journal is a good way to bring the inner experiences of healing into the here and now. Your journal entries create a map of your healing work, and reading it later will serve to remind you of the many milestones of your healing progress.

Some people prefer to purchase an elaborate blank book to use as a journal. These are available from gift or book stores. However, any type of plain notebook can become your Spiritual Journal.

For your first entry, begin by writing the questions that will guide your spiritual understanding of the people in your life. Leave plenty room between questions to fill in thoughts that you have about each person.

Ask:

1. Why did I plan from the spiritual realm to be involved with (fill in name)?

2. What am I to learn from (fill in name)?

3. What kind of love am I experiencing?

4. Did I give or receive something unique?

5. What will I take forth into my own spirit?

This exercise will help to deepen your understanding of the roles of the many people in your life. It need not only refer to those who have died. Use this to realize your connection to people, places, and events throughout your life. You will begin to see patterns of interaction that give great meaning to your spiritual journey.

Keeping a Spiritual Journal is a task of love and a record to be cherished. Keep it private so that you have greater freedom to write your most intimate thoughts and feelings. Use it to monitor your progress, to hold your fears until you can let them go completely, and to save your healing messages.

6

Grieving the Death of Mother

Understanding Mother and letting her go

None of us can remember how we got into our body from the spiritual world. Mother is our link between here and there. She is an integral part of our connection to Spirit. There is a special spiritual part of our brain that comes from our biological Mother. Whether we were given up for adoption, or lost our Mother early in life, we carry her with us every moment of every day. We carry "Mother" in the memories of our cells. We have an unbreakable tie to her.

Our spiritual and emotional ties to Mother come from three very unique sources: cellular-memory; direct or indirect experience of Mother; and, the expectation that we have about what a Mother is, compared to our own.

Cellular memory is sometimes called our spiritual genes and is not the same as thoughts or old pictures. It does not recall times, dates, and places. Cellular memory is made up of the parts of our emotional memory experiences that have no words. It is also the way the body remembers what the mind experiences.

Every feeling we ever have during every moment of our life, from the very instant the first cell of our body began to form, is stored forever in all our cells. Much of that information is from Mother's experiences when we were still in her womb. These experiences are transmitted from Mother to child-from her Mother to her, and all the Mothers before her. This link to her, and all the generations that came before her, is always present and stays with each of us for our lifetime. It is our special connection to Mother's Spirit and Mother's love that never leaves us.

One of the ways that we experience Mother's love is through our emotional connection and her acts of Mothering. The way Mom takes care of us during infancy and childhood forms the framework for how we experience our greatest pleasures and triumphs, or worst negative feelings and attitudes that can cut us off from a great source of unconditional love for the rest of life.

As I have seen so many times in my work, how well we are able to tap into our spiritual self often depends on how well we understand the spiritual and emotional ties of these precious relationships.

The death of Mother is only one of the many ways that you experience her loss during the course of a lifetime. Some people experience the loss of Mother at birth, either through her death, or through adoption. Others experience abandonment through growth and change brought on by personal development, or unavoidable circumstances like divorce or financial crises. The loss of Mother in any way can bring feelings and beliefs that everyone you love, and everyone who loves you, will eventually leave, just like Mom.

When she is unable to fulfill our need for love, we look for copies of her in many relationships. We seek the love and acceptance that we did not receive from her, in work, play, and home in ways that leave us empty and desperate - always feeling cut off from the Mother Love that we all so desperately need. Healing the loss of Mother requires that we understand the special nature of the Mother Spirit.

The soul that chooses to become "Mom" is choosing to grow through a life of hardship and pain. However, every Mom has a Mother, who had a Mother, who had a Mother, for thousands of years. Each of us is the holder of the precious centuries of "Mother's Love" that is passed on and into us. The answer to the questions and the mystery of Mother's Love lies, not with Mom, but within the spiritual self of your soul.

Breaking the strong earth-bound ties with Mother takes more than the precious closure of a funeral or the inner quiet of meditation. When Mom dies, she creates an opportunity for you to grow. You are transformed by her transformation. She makes the transition back to the spiritual world from which she came, leaving you to find the secret of Mother's Love. You must also make a transition. You must let her go if you are to find it. Letting go of the earth-bound ties to her means that you become aware of the ultimate source of unconditional love from Mother's Love that allows you to transform with her.

You can stop making her be "Mother." You can stop blaming her for all your faults and failings. Let go of each sad event that challenged you along your early path. This release means freedom to create a state of grace and an eternal connection between the Mother's Spirit and Mother's Love that is so much greater than what you can imagine her to be. You are commanded to grow on your own.

The Mother Spirit will come to earth many more times and repeat the circle of life in many different bodies. Each time she leaves behind wisdom for you to learn through grieving her loss and healing your grief: "Your life must be your own and you must allow yourself to be changed with the death of Mom."

This is the commandment of Mother's Spirit. Let's look at some of the ways that we see our relationship to Mother so that we can begin to understand our spiritual relationship to Mother and begin to release her.

Everybody has an ideal Mother, the fantasy of the perfect Mother. Somewhere in your mind you seek the perfect person who is ultimately Mother. You expect more than just feelings and reactions from your ideal Mom. You seek her total and unconditional love and acceptance throughout your lifetime. You weave fantasies that are always bigger than Mom because you expect so much from her.

Mom is supposed to be the ultimate nurturer. She is the one who would always be there, always have the best advice, and always know the right thing to do. If Mom said you would be happily married, you believed her. If Mom said you should trust someone, you trusted. Mom was never supposed to be tired, busy, or wrong.

Often, you see her as the "Supreme Being" who has the power to comfort, feed, and shelter you, both physically and emotionally. Her love can guide you safely and tenderly through your early journey or, if withdrawn, can send you out into the world feeling frightened and hungry.

Sometimes because of our expectations, we create fantasy images of Mom. In the "Super Mom" fantasy, you create the perfect Mom. A typical conventional fantasy of the perfect Super Mom is one who gets up early to make breakfast, packs her children off to school with a healthy, neatly packed lunch, then goes to a high-paying job that lets her get home before they return from school.

The Super Mom's house is always clean and the laundry is always done. Dinner is always healthy and delicious and dessert is always something fresh and wonderful - made from scratch, of course. The kids can call her at work whenever they need her. She stays home and gives them her undivided attention when they get sick. She's never too busy for PTA meetings, sports games or recitals. She makes special treats when their friends come over. Her advice is always wise and given with tender love. When her children grow up, she, naturally, loves their marriage choice. She's the best of Grandmothers, and supports her children in every life and career decision they may make.

Each one of us weaves fantasies of Super Mom and interacts with it throughout our lives. When we begin to understand the spiritual nature of our relationship to her, we can bear the pain of her loss and find the true Mother in our own spirit. As we grow in understanding the real Mother Spirit, we are able to release her from our fantasies, and cut the emotional strings that keep us from moving along our healing journey.

When Mom dies, you know she will never fulfill our "Super Mom" dreams. An even harsher and more frightening thought is that YOU will not be able to live up to any of your dreams.

You may think, "If all-powerful Mom couldn't do it, how can I?"

When this thought takes hold of you, you feel as though all your hopes are shattered. You begin to question your worth and place in the Divine plan: "How can I possibly be what Mom wanted me to be if she was just another human being herself?"

Everyone has had these questions from time to time. These thoughts can make you feel betrayed, as though Mom has somehow broken her promise to you. You may feel you will never be able to live up to what she wanted from you now that she's gone. In grieving Mother, these questions begin to nag us, tear at our souls, tear our self-esteem apart, and undermine our confidence:

> "Maybe I did not accomplish enough before she died?"

> "Did I earn enough money?"

> "If only I had gotten more education . . . "

> "Am I the Mother that Mom was?"

> "She was the one who gave me life, and now her loss threatens to take it away."

> "How will I survive?"

The unanswerable questions continue until we replace them with those that give a deeper understanding. If these questions are plaguing you, know that you can dispel them. Turn to your Spiritual Journal and begin to replace them with those that help you see her from your spirit.

Sometimes when we lose Mom, we feel that we have lost a link to love and perhaps even our path to God. If this is your experience, it is understandable that you feel angry and fretful. You may even rail against her death and retreat into darkness and total abandonment like a child with no comfort. Feeling lost, you secretly search for her, yearn for her, get angry at her. You question your chances for success in love, happiness, and ability to grow:

> "How can I ever reach my own soul without her?"

> "Where can I find the love I need?"

You may become so lost and confused when Mom dies that you think you have no right to keep living. Know that you can survive and live a successful life. You can love and have joy and happiness. Even though you may strive to become exactly like Mom, hoping to capture and hold some part of her here on earth as a way of holding on to her, you do not have to keep Mom's spirit alive in your own body. She is available to you through cellular memories and your own unique connection to her spirit and love.

We go through a lot when Mom dies. Often, we relive our entire lives in memories. Sometimes we blame her for all our character flaws, our mistakes, and our bad feelings because we know that she is strong enough to take it. We may even try to justify our growth pains by reasoning that because we came into the body through hers, SHE must be the reason we feel betrayed, ashamed, deprived or empty. Some unhappy people are never able to discern which of their feelings come from "Mother" or themselves. They are never able to separate from her or become confused about which memories are hers and which are their own, still experiencing life through Mother's memories. In body, we long for the comfort and safety of her arms as though we were in her womb again.

Review the Mother's Commandment: "Your life must be your own and you must allow yourself to be changed with my transition."

It is a call to action to heal by deciding that your life is your own. You begin the process of separating what Mom gave you from your own experiences. As you exercise your awareness of your spiritual self, you take steps to release Mom from her earth-bound role. Allow her to go finish her cycle in the spiritual world while you tend to your own.

No matter who Mom is, or what you think she did to you, your soul chose this person to be Mother. This was one of the decisions you made at the beginning of your own choice to be her child from the spirit realm.

When you look at the best and the worst of

Mom, you must look with love and compassion.

As you begin the process of deciding what is Mom and what is authentically your own, begin to say:

> "I no longer accept this idea that came from Mom," or "I want to keep this part of what Mom gave me."

Begin to examine your thoughts, feelings, reactions, and give yourself permission to change without guilt. Let's begin with how you think about Mother. Does she mean life, love, and happiness to you? Does she mean blame, sickness, anger, and punishment?

If you think of Mom as angry or hurtful, you may focus on those feelings when she dies. This kind of focus can be so self-destructive that it gets in the way of your day-to-day life. It interferes with how and why you separate from her in healthy growth. You must cut the strings to these negative feelings before you can cut your strings to Mom.

It may take time to fully understand your grief and loss of her. You may be surprised at how deep and strong your emotional and spiritual ties are to her. You may even begin to look at Spirit differently. Many people begin to embrace the feminine side of God as the heart opens through understanding Mother's spirit.

Think about why you chose this woman to be your Mother. What did she teach you? Did you learn well? Did she grow because of you? As you begin to think about these questions, remember that you chose her from your spiritual place in the ethereal for very important reasons. No matter what may have happened throughout your relationship to her before her death, you needed this particular person in your life, whether only for birth time, a brief time, or a long time. The answers are within the memories she passed into you.

Making these choices fills your mind and spirit with your own thoughts and wants. You begin to accept that Mom's path does not control your journey. You give yourself permission to explore your own power in mind and spirit. You realize that life is a gift and Spirit is always with you.

When you truly know that Mother's Spirit is separate from yours, you experience a new happiness and hope. You cut the symbolic umbilical once more and Mother's love floods you as you direct your own future and dream your own dreams. Self-directed dreams of Mother are one of the many ways that we begin to see her. Dare to dream your own dreams.

Psychologists say the dreams we have while we are asleep come from our subconscious mind. We all have them every night, even if we do not always remember them. If we did not dream, we would not survive. We do not have any direct input into these kinds of dreams. To control our dreams, we have to meditate. This will slow brain movement so we can see the symbols of the spiritual self. This technique of spiritual awareness is called actualization.

Actualization is a way of visualizing the spirit through our own link into the spiritual world from our soul. These symbols become the blueprint that will seep into our consciousness awareness and guide us. The way to Mother's love is through our eternal link to Mother's Spirit. We are connected to that link through our self-directed spirit dreams. Meditation can help us rediscover our link to her and heal the grief that binds us.

Healing Meditation

Actualizing Mother

This meditation is designed to help us begin to actualize Mother's love.

It can be helpful for you to play some soft instrumental music that makes you feel relaxed, and gives you a sense of peace and inner quiet. You will need recorded music the length of the meditation.

To experience the maximum benefits of this exercise, you also need a timer, a journal or notebook that you can use for personal writing, and a pen.

Set the timer for 20 minutes if you prefer the shortest meditation, or 40 minutes for the longer experience. You decide what is most comfortable.

Turn on your relaxation music. Place your journal and pen beside you so that you do not have to rise to get them. Set the timer for the desired time.

If at all possible, go to your sacred space where you will not be interrupted, and find a comfortable sitting position.

Close your eyes. Feel your mind begin to leave the business of the day behind.

Drop your shoulders. Feel your body begin to let go of its burden as you notice a comfortable easiness move through you. Take a deep breath. Exhale. Feel the release.

As you exhale, begin to feel the tensions of the day blow gently away from you. Imagine yourself being caressed by a sweet sea breeze that flows around you and carries your tensions away on your breath. Allow yourself to follow your breath toward the ocean and imagine your body floating on a gentle ocean wave. Feel the breeze take the tension away from you with each breath. Feel the tensions of your body wash out to sea, away from you as you float smoothly and steadily on top of the wave.

Relax. Feel a deep rocking sensation. Relax into feelings of complete safety and security.

Let your mind drift into the quiet, into that special deep place where you can feel the safety and comfort of your favorite place to be alone. Let it begin to form in your mind. It might be lying under the stars or on the fresh green grass of a meadow, floating on the ocean, or resting in the sun. Go to this familiar place right now.

Breathe deeply, evenly. Feel the preciousness of this place. When you are ready, begin to see a large screen like a movie screen in this special place.

As the screen emerges a movie begins. It is the movie of your adult memories of Mom.

Feel the love, the peacefulness, and the grandness all around you. Tell yourself that you will remember all the things that you are seeing on the screen. All the things that you see on the screen are important to you. Take your time. Do not try to force it. Be patient and allow the deep images to come forth.

When you hear the timer take a deep breathe and open your eyes. Slowly, sit up without getting up, and pick up your journal and pen.

While the images are still fresh in your mind's eye, begin to look at what you saw. Write down all of Mom's good and bad points that you saw on the big screen. Write down all the things you like and those that bothered you.

Put stars or bullets beside the things that have special meaning for you.

Allow your emotions to flow as you write. When you have finished, close the journal and take a deep breath. Exhale forcefully, and let go. Congratulate yourself for your courage and appreciation of life. Put your journal in a private place so that your freedom to write is not disturbed.

This exercise helps you begin to see yourself as separate from Mom. It also helps you begin to see who she really was. It is the first step in loosening the emotional strings and exercising your spiritual self across the connection to Mother's Love.

Your spiritual self can seek the shelter of Mother's love at any time! That ever-present font of unending Mother's love abides in your body, mind, and spirit. It is unconditional and unending.

With practice, you will say, "I love you, and no love ever dies. Goodbye," and "May we meet at the fountain of Mother's Love where we are each renewed throughout our journey."

A Mother is a very strong emotional presence. There are so many emotions connected to the Mother because she is the first source of survival and nurturing that you receive on this Earth plane.

There are many people that blame their Mothers for the problems in their lives. I understand this, because I know that Mother is the creatrix of life. Mother is the bridge that brought our soul to this world. However, if you cannot forgive your Mother, you cannot forgive yourself.

When you make peace with your Mother, you free yourself to dream your own dream. Whether you feel as though you didn't do enough for her or she didn't do enough for you, this is the time to forgive. Acknowledge, forgive, and change to release the burden of negative thoughts. If you don't make peace, you'll end up moving from one phase to another in your life with the negativity continuing.

You have to acknowledge this inside to make your world a happy place. By forgiving your Mother, you take back the power to nurture yourself.

Grieving the Death of Father

Understanding the role of Father

Having loved my Father dearly, I knew my life was going to change dramatically when he made his transition.

It was a week after my Father had passed when I sat in my sacred space talking to Spirit. I asked "Now, where do I belong?" It was only four hours later when my good friend John White called me and asked "Are you ready to come to Lily Dale?" The answer had come. Yes, I was ready. This shifted my life from living in Florida year round to sharing half the year in upstate New York.

Within a few weeks of arriving in Lily Dale, I encountered my Father's spirit stronger than ever. I told him "Yes, Dad I know you're with me here." He said to me, "Patti this is where you belong."

In my willingness to bring my Father's spirit closer to me, I found the next step on my journey. For some people this is a total transformation; for others it's a minor adjustment to their lives.

Having a sense of security is vital to our survival and growth throughout our life. When we feel safe and secure, we are able to grow and develop without the stress and worry of threats to our survival. Our strength and self-sufficiency emerges as we learn the tools necessary to make our way in this world. Traditionally, in western society, we acquire this kind of knowledge from Father or the masculine aspect of the parent providing the protection and security.

Social expectations of men and women are vastly different. Usually, it is the male and Father that is cast in the role of "provider" and "protector." It is expected of men that they work to support their families in a home and social environment in which their children can thrive.

There is no doubt that the relationship between Fathers and daughters and Fathers and sons is vastly different. How we express our masculine and feminine aspects takes many forms throughout our lifetime. We do not recognize or manifest our masculine or feminine sides by making a conscious decision to set such a goal. It usually happens subconsciously and without our acknowledgement.

A good example of this is how girls and boys play differently. Although society has different expectations and beliefs about gender roles, experiments have proven, in short, that girls "create" and boys "provide" in terms of home and family. This is in no way to say that these roles cannot be interchangeable. However, the masculine dominant role is to protect and provide and the feminine dominant role is to create and nurture.

When Father dies, issues of security become the focus for the surviving family members. Even adult children experience thoughts about security and strength as those issues relate to their own family, or perhaps their grandchildren. The loss of Father may bring feelings of helplessness or fears that make us feel exposed to the world or more vulnerable than usual.

It is common for sons and daughters to experience their deep connection to male energy through dreams that have to do with issues of physical safety and financial security. Sometimes people dream of losing their job or of being lost and unable to find their way back home. We may experience a sense of preciousness associated with meeting our daily needs. Little things may become extremely important.

When Father makes his transition, it is assumed that the son will assume the role and responsibilities of protection and security. Sons identify more strongly with the male attributes of Father. A son may silently inherit Father's role or experience a "passing of the mantle" that acknowledges his manhood when Father dies.

When there are many males in a family their roles and responsibilities within and to the family will be silently assigned or conveyed. The expectations a Father has of his male children forms an impression of roles and responsibilities that follow the child all of his life.

For sons and daughters this sense of empowerment also comes with concerns about self-confidence, true readiness, and worthiness to walk in Father's footsteps.

A son may question, "Am I going to be able to do it like my Father did?"

"Do I want to do it like Dad did?"

"Can I live up to his expectations and those of the family?"

He may feel inadequate and fear that he will "never be a real man like his Father."

A daughter may feel that she has her Father's super strength and attempt to do "everything that a man can do." However, she may secretly be trying to prove herself to her Father, who is no longer there to help her integrate his masculine strength into her feminine role in a healthy way.

Daughters may look more inward than sons for their identification with Father. They also want to be able to see themselves in Father's eyes and consider his expectations of her.

"Did he expect her to be beautiful?"

"Did he expect her to be talented?"

"Did he expect her to marry and stay at home or work on a career as well?"

When there are no sons, and the daughter has been the focus of Father's strength, she may amplify her masculine traits and overcompensate in assuming his role after his death. She may, in essence, try to do it all.

While striving to learn about the masculine and feminine aspects of our personalities and how those roles are a healthy complement in life, sons and daughters may fear stereotypes of "too masculine" or "too feminine" at times in the grieving process.

Making adjustments to the permanent change brought on by Father's death requires that we become aware of how gender roles affect our perceptions about who and what we are. The kind of relationship that you had with your Father and the role that he filled in your family determines how you may be affected when he dies.

The traditional Father is sometimes called "the forgotten parent." Although today men are accepted in delivery rooms, expected to participate in birthing and parenting classes, have greater custody rights, and more overall responsibilities for child-care, in many cases, Fathers are not as active in daily child-rearing as mothers. Dad is not expected to be the nurturing parent, but rather the stronghold for the family. It is his strength, assurance, influence, presence, and energy that protects mother so that she can create and express all that she desires for her family, and have the freedom to nurture them.

Mother teaches us to do internal problem solving and gives us confidence in who and what we are. From Mother we learn emotional depth and expressive language, and how to develop our internal world. Father, in his equal contribution, is the parent who teaches us to use tools and problem solve in the world so that our ability to provide for ourselves gives us confidence.

When Father dies the impact is profound. It is a time when we examine the past and try to peer into the future and consider what part of him we take with us. There is no such thing as a perfect life. There is no such person as the perfect parent. The most important thing to remember as you work through grief is to embrace acceptance and forgiveness. Make a sincere effort towards forgiveness towards your parents for all their perceived shortcomings.

Forgive yourself for the times when you did not "measure up" or fell short of your Father's hopes for you. Forgive yourself for all the little things that stick in the mind, like the things we wish we had said or done and didn't for whatever reason at the time. Forgive yourself for all the unexpressed, inappropriate or over-reactive emotions and simply say, "I'm sorry."

Accept that you were the best son or daughter that you could possibly be by realizing that we are all imperfect. Give yourself permission to heal physically, mentally, and spiritually.

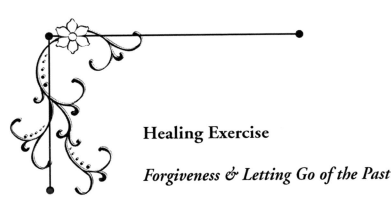

Healing Exercise

Forgiveness & Letting Go of the Past

Use your sacred space to perform these exercises. Be aware of the energy that your space holds. Acknowledge that it is a place of freedom, privacy, and respect for the work that you are doing in healing grief.

Forgiveness is a light that burns bright in the soul of each of us. It is a burning away and clearing of the negative thoughts and feelings that have bound us through fear and pain.

The purpose of this exercise is to open your mind and heart to the power of forgiveness to release you from the shackles of the past. You will need a large and beautiful, long burning candle, preferably white (to symbolize the light of forgiveness that lives in the soul and its eternal connection to Divine Love).

Each day, for seven days light the candle and say a prayer of forgiveness. These simple words are more than sufficient:

"I forgive myself for all those I may have
injured in thought, word, or deed."

"I let go of the anger and pain
and invite peace, wisdom and understanding
to fill my heart, soul, and mind."

"I open myself to forgiveness
so that it may surround me."

"I invite forgiveness to free me from the past
so that I can create a new future
filled with positive emotions."

"I know that I am truly forgiven
and restored in love."

You may find it helpful to make a list of the people who come into your mind that you believe you have hurt or who have caused you pain.

Release them one at a time by saying:

"I forgive myself and _____(insert their name), and I set us free."

In this way, you are giving new life to that person and filling your own with positive energy.

If there are events that you hold in your memory that you would like to release and receive forgiveness for, speak those times and visualize them going into the bright light of the candle forever.

With the image of Father in your mind, close this exercise by saying:

"May love and joy be yours and mine as we walk our paths in this lifetime."

You can use this Forgiveness Exercise with many people and events throughout your life.

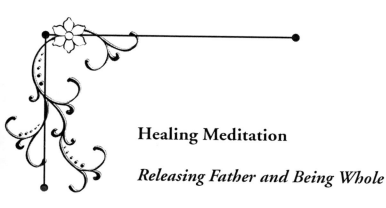

Healing Meditation

Releasing Father and Being Whole

Return to your sacred space and find a comfortable sitting position.

Sit with your legs uncrossed as you begin to breathe deeply, slowly, feeling the tension begin to leave your body.

Allow yourself to drift on your breath as you continue to breathe deeply and evenly.

Feel the tension leave your face and neck. Feel your shoulders drop, relaxed as the tension leaves your back. Feel your thighs release and your legs feel heavy all the way down to your toes, until you feel completely relaxed and safely drifting in peace.

As you drift, imagine a beautiful white light that begins to move toward you. Feel yourself drift into this light. Feel the warmth and allow a sense of total security to wash over and through you. The light releases all your anxiety and worry.

Surrounded by the light, you feel yourself begin to float higher and higher, letting go of the world beneath you. You feel the light carrying you, holding you safely in peace.

Begin to form an image of a beautiful place in your mind. As you float on the light, you begin to see the image more clearly. It is a beautiful place of green trees and a babbling brook. You realize that the light has carried you to this pristine place, and you lie down beside a lake of crystal water.

Slowly look into the water and see someone beside you. It is your Father. You know him completely, with a sense of familiarity that is deeper than you have ever experienced before. You feel total acceptance.

In this state of complete knowing, you begin to talk to him with honesty and openness from your heart and soul.

Tell him about all your childhood angers and disappointments.

Describe your hopes and dreams and ambitions.

Talk about who you really are and what he really means to you.

Tell him about all the times you felt ignored, discounted, invisible, left out.

Tell him all the things that fear has kept you from saying.

Tell him how much you needed him and wanted his love.

See that your Father is really listening to you with all his spirit, heart, and soul focused on who you really are.

Feel his acceptance. Feel his forgiveness. Then you begin show him how proud he can be of you now.

Tell him how strong you are and proud you are of your own accomplishments. Let him know that you have become a capable and talented adult with your own ideas, life, family, and job.

Tell him how you are different from him and how you are the same. As you are talking, you realize that your Father has asked you for forgiveness for his failures, and shortcomings. You can see his eyes acknowledge your words.

As you and your Father are talking, you realize that both of you accept your differences and begin to celebrate them by laughing together. You have spoken your failures and imperfections and celebrate that you are both limited by life on this earth, but in spirit all things are possible.

Feel the Divine Love that surrounds you and fills you. As you sit beside him in this beautiful place make this a sacred time with him. Know that you are letting go of all the pain and replacing it with forgiveness and acceptance and love that has been bound by negative thoughts.

Thank him for giving you life. Tell him that it is okay for him to go and that you understand that you too, must walk your path alone. Remember that you chose him as your Father from a place that you do not remember. Let him know that his job is done and your lessons are yours to take into your own journey.

Before you part, visualize your Father as he hands you a gift. It is a symbol of all that you have shared. It represents a new depth of understanding, and appreciation of how you have healed each other.

Thank him for all that you have shared. See the light that surrounds you move to surround him and carry him higher and higher from this sacred place.

As you watch him move into the clouds, step into the crystal water and walk out into the middle of the pool, feeling it bathe your soul, wash all worries from your mind, cleansing you, renewing you, healing you of all pain.

Relax and begin to float on the water. Let the healing water carry you to the shore where you feel the warm earth beneath you. As the water recedes, feel the warmth of the sun begin to dry your skin. A gentle breeze moves across your face as you move to sit up, to stand.

See a tall, strong tree in the distance and begin to walk to the tree. Feel the strength of its roots from deep beneath the cool earth holding it straight and steady.

As you sit beneath the tree and look upward at its boughs and broad limbs your chest fills with peace and comfort. Close your eyes in sweet sleep and know that you can return to this sacred place at any time.

Begin to count backwards from five . . . four . . . three . . . two . . . one.

When you are ready, open your eyes and feel the healing power.

Know that you are all that you want to be, that your ambitions, dreams, hopes, and wishes are yours to create because you have created this opportunity to look at Father and tell him that you love him.

Take this lesson into all your relationships. You are strong, courageous, and creative. Through Divine Love you have learned to love yourself, and trust in that love to make all things new.

Grieving the Loss of a Child

When God calls His children, we have no choice but to let them go. Though mortality interrupts our hope, it collects unfinished dreams and sends them onward on the wings of Spirit, to be reunited in the next circle of life. Our children are not our destiny. We are only the doorways in which children are able to come into this world to fulfill what they need to do in this earth plane. The healing journey following the loss of a child is a special one. It is a journey that begins with grace, followed by forgiveness, and understanding.

The loss of a child is not like any other form of grief. The pain seems almost unbearable. When a child dies, there is a sinking feeling, like your own internal life is oozing out into the void. So many times, we make our children the vessel of our own hopes and dreams. All our wishes for our own life are placed upon them. More than in any other loss, the death of a child seems to also terminate our hopes and dreams for ourselves. Seemingly, it is the end of our investment in this lifetime, but there is a deeper purpose for them and for us.

When we look at mothers and children together, we see the transfer of all that came before, the inheritance of all that Mother's love and spirit bore into the child. This can include dreams as well as pain. Our children mirror our lives. We see our own life stages in them.

Often we ask questions of our own experiences:

"Was I a happy child?"

"How am I going to change things for MY child?"

"What can he or she have that I could not?"

"What can I fix that was not fixed in me?"

"How can I love when I was not loved?"

"How can I protect and nurture this new life to be better than my own?"

We use these questions to compensate for our own feelings of inadequacy as parents and to make up for the things we did not get or could not change as children. These questions, and our unexamined answers, carry the parent's hopes and dreams into the child as well as pain and sorrow.

Sometimes we live through our children. Many ideas, unfulfilled wishes, and unspoken emotional contracts are placed on children prior to their birth that are not their own. All of these things go into becoming a parent. We cannot escape the self-examination and comparison that we go through from our own lives to that of our children.

When a child dies, we are left with an overwhelming sense of failure: "If I had only been a better person, a better parent, this never would have happened."

No matter how the loss occurs, the guilt and blame is the same. There are no good words to express the grief. Communication vanishes between spouses, parents and other children, and other family and friends. Often the only bond that remains is the pain and silence.

Grief's hold can be so strong that parents cannot act for themselves, and must be surrounded by those who can guide them swiftly into a place of emotional safety and security. There is a need for help from many different sources for strength, protection, and even support for the day-to-day chores of living. Continuous therapies may be needed to guide the powerful transformation from grief into a new life.

It takes special spiritual guidance to understand the differences between the mother and father connection to the child. The pain of the loss of a child through death is an ugly and unrelenting taskmaster that must be released with special understanding of the maternal bond.

There is no greater imprint on a Mother's soul or psyche than the loss of a child. What special gift of strength or spirit could possibly endure? What wisdom could rise above the wretchedness and writhing to reveal a Higher Self, when only one question lingers: "Why?"

The maternal connection is the most complex. When a child dies, the mother's maternal energy becomes so intensified, and leaves her with such force and power as if it can no longer be housed within her. It explodes out into the universe in search of the child it was bound to surround, protect, and heal. This energy is so powerful; it will sacrifice the mother's life force in an attempt to fulfill its duties.

To save the woman and release the child, it is necessary to interrupt the maternal connection to the child through the mother's mind. It is a time to call upon the body to keep the mind and spirit in the "here and now", connected to appetites, stimulation, and contact with our external environment.

It is maternal energy that fuels intuition, protection, and healing of both mother and child. When the spirit of the child enters the transition to death, this energy seeks to pull back into a realm that no longer needs it. Detaching the intuitive connection from this child is an extremely difficult process because we cannot remember our own detachment from the spiritual realm into the earthly one.

Because there are no words that are capable of expressing this grief, pain often becomes the common bond between the parents.

As a result of the great pain associated with the loss of a child, parents may feel such a great burden that they end up separating physically, emotionally, or both. Many may feel an additional sense of guilt as though they could have done more. Other parents may feel like their reason for being together is no longer. If there are surviving children, these burdens get passed onto the entire household.

When a child dies, we need to recognize each other's suffering and recognize that each individual expresses their pain in their own unique manner.

Our children are our wishes, hopes, and dreams. When you lose a child you lose a piece of that dream.

How do you say goodbye?

How do you integrate this experience into your lives and keep going?

There are no quick and easy answers in this process. There are no simple solutions. Though every moment is a trip to eternity when you instinctively seek that child, know that God's plan holds a deeper meaning for you.

By looking at your own relationship to your child, and your parents to you, you begin to get a glimpse of a universal secret that is inherent in our parent-child cycle of life. Whether the child is 7 days, 7 months, 7 years, or aged 70, you begin to look at what these precious ones mean in your life and begin to separate your dreams and hopes about their lives from their own destiny.

You dreamed a dream for them on this earth. You had hopes and wishes for them here.

Now you must dream the dream and create a hope and wishes for them elsewhere. Creating the dream of their transition and freedom, of their ability to be happy, to laugh, to play, and know that they are whole in returning to their perfect spiritual state.

Healing the pain from the loss of a child has a lot to do with understanding how much the mother or father identified with the stages of their child's life. For example, the memories that we have as an infant are reflected in our own child's infancy. Throughout their growth, although it may seem that we had forgotten most of our own, we become flooded with memories of what we did, said, and thought when we were the ages of our child. If we can recognize that we do this, we can uncover our own emotional agenda that we may have cast onto the life of our child. We can look deeper into our own experiences and in so doing, release them into their transition.

As you begin to realize your own emotional ages and stages and separate them from those of your child you will recognize the child's own spiritual essence and the charge of their own destiny. Our dreams now function to bring us wholeness, to correct our misperceptions, and to establish physical arid emotional health and restore balance. We must recreate our own dreams-those for our own life.

Often we begin to realize that we had strong feelings of shame, guilt, fears, old anger that were never released or worked through as we grew into adulthood. We carry these powerful feelings inside of us and keep them alive just under the surface of our relationships with our own children. In some instances, we can even uncover patterns of shaming, irrational fears, or other strong negative, possibly even destructive feelings that get passed from our parents to us and from us to our children.

The intensity of these emotions and the sweeping power of these patterns can cause us to be paralyzed in the grieving process. Thoughts and feelings that may have been dormant for decades can awaken and burst out into your life triggered by this terrible crisis time.

This transformation time presents you with the opportunity to heal generations of patterns, feelings, thoughts, and dreams that serve to release your child into this transition, and fill the void with peace, serenity, and love that can transcend generations in your family. Though God has forgiven each of us as we struggle together to learn about love and spirit, we may not have forgiven ourselves.

Healing Exercise

Prayer for your child

Creating the dream of your child's transition

Go to your sacred space where you will not be interrupted. Find a comfortable sitting position. Some people like to create a cushion from a folded blanket or pillow and kneel for this exercise.

Close your eyes. Feel your mind begin to leave the business of the day behind.

Drop your shoulders. Feel your body begin to let go of its burden as you notice a comfortable easiness move through you.

Take a deep breath. Exhale. Feel the release.

Take another deep breath, and imagine that you are breathing the breath of God, that He is so close to you, surrounding you. You begin to feel His warmth in your heart, recognize His peace in your mind.

Slowly, let thoughts of gratitude fill your mind. Let the thoughts float upward on the Grace that surrounds you. Gently floating from the top of your head into the breath of God, imagine your thoughts light as the air.

Begin to silently pray. If you cannot think of a prayer, say the simple words, "I love you, God. Blessed Divine, fill me with your love and give me strength and courage." Begin to pray for your child.

As you pray for this child, visualize handing her/him over into the gentle hands of Spirit. Allow the tears to flow and the grieving to occur. Ask Spirit to remain close that you may know the peace and serenity of your child in the perfect spiritual state. See that child sparkle with the light of God. Listen as Spirit whispers to you, "Your child is safe. Your child is filled with Divine Love. Your child blesses you and releases you to complete your life."

Ask that your life continue to be filled with the love that that Spirit has shown you, the love that God has for your child. Allow Spirit to show you that this child is completely protected, nurtured, and alive in Divine Love.

Release your maternal power to transcend its needs and restore its integrity by placing her child into the hands of God. Ask this power to return to you in peace and assurance of God's greater plan.

Prayer is the most outstanding source of intimate comfort for all people in spiritual crisis. People who pray gain strength, courage, and an understanding of their place in the Universe. Whether it is through prayer, meditation, or private moments of silence and reflection on the life of this child, we begin to restructure our hopes and dreams in God's trust.

Healing Exercise

Loving and Letting Go

Our dreams and hopes and wishes for our children begin with a quick journey and exquisite wholeness in his or her perfect spiritual state. One way to manifest this is to create what is called a prayer flag.

The prayer flag is unique to your child and who he or she was on earth. It can be as simple as a piece of cloth on which you draw with fabric markers, or as complex as a hand sewn banner.

Whatever you chose to create, it is a precious symbol of this spirit on earth, for however brief or long that may have been. It does not need to be elaborate. You may want to include a favorite passage, tie on a small picture, or create felt figures or flowers that can be glued onto the flag. It is the love that infuses this flag that makes it special.

As you work with this piece, use your thoughts of love to let go of the child's spirit.

Imagine the spirit frolicking in a field of flowers.

Silently think: "I love this child and set it free. From within my heart I release the dreams, hopes, and wishes, knowing that this flag flies high and will fly on the winds, the spirit of this child moves as the flag moves."

When you are finished, fly the flag and speak the words aloud.

"Let children walk with Nature,
let them see the beautiful blendings
and communions of death and life,
their joyous inseparable unity,
as taught in woods and meadows,
plains and mountains and streams of
our blessed star, and they will learn
that death is stingless indeed,
and as beautiful as life."

John Muir
(1838–1914) naturalist
founder of the Sierra Club

9

Helping Children Deal With Grief

When children are in touch with nature and animals, especially in rural areas, they begin to understand the grief process earlier. However, in today's information age, children are not having this experience, and therefore are asking more questions and wanting deeper answers. Children want to know where their love goes. For example, they might ask "I still love my brother, can I still love him? Can I love my father?"

One summer in Lily Dale, a five year old girl was brought to me by her mother. The little girl had recently lost her father, and was telling her mother that she was still able to communicate with him. Through her innocent eyes, she felt like she could feel her father's presence and see him. This is why we need to be aware of the fact that children in their innocence can communicate with spirit. She was able to console her mother that her father was ok, and that he was watching out for them.

When we are talking to children about death, we need to allow them to participate in these conversations, and not put them on the sidelines. We need to respect their emotional intelligence.

Children need support, guidance, and a special understanding when they experience the loss of someone they love. When families experience death, often it is the children who are left out of the grieving and healing process because the parents are devastated by the loss and unable to help their children.

It is important to understand how children experience loss and grief. Most children do not perceive death with the same finality that adults do. However, they certainly do feel the impact. Their experience is dominated by a constant sense of separation. Sometimes children interpret this as abandonment, rejection, and guilt-possibly even as their fault because the scope of the crisis and total changes in the household cannot be grasped.

Children do not have much of an opportunity to change things that impact their world. Therefore, the effect of loss and the consequent changes in the household may cause them to feel indifferent, confused, or even abandoned. They may act out with oppositional behaviors or completely withdraw because they do not have the ability to regulate their emotions.

In addition to the need for professional help and support from teachers, ministers, and other people in your community, there are a few simple things that you can be aware of when dealing with a child who is grieving.

It is always better to acknowledge the effect of losing a loved one on all those in the household than to pretend that nothing has changed. A child's intuition is pure and very sensitive. They have levels of awareness that they have no words to describe. They know and feel the impact and may keep it silent. Bring it out into the environment. Help the child to find the right words for the feelings. Help the child to express behaviors that match the feelings that they cannot comprehend.

People mistakenly believe that talking honestly and openly about death makes it worse. They may not know what to say or how to speak about these feelings to a child. It could be because as adults we do not remember what the mind of a child is like, or it could be that we are the ones unable to deal with the situation. Do not be afraid to tell your child the truth. Many parents think that children cannot handle it. That is a mistake! Children instinctively know the truth and recognize betrayal.

When truth is circumvented "for the sake of the child", it leaves a feeling of distrust or betrayal. The child becomes confused and even more helpless to find a place in the changed world. I am not suggesting that you lay out details for children, keep the information brief and to the point.

As adults, we use a lot of words, images, and symbols in our thoughts and conversations. Children want simple, straight answers. Always speak to them in age-appropriate language using representations that they can relate to. Be creative but never give them too much information. You can see the child withdraw or get lost in the information when you say too much. Keep it sensitive, brief and exactly relevant to their questions.

Sometimes children need to ask the same questions over and over. This is usually when they are struggling with the change or have trouble grasping the information. Allow them to ask as often as they need to. Don't talk down to them. Remember to treat their feelings with tenderness and compassion. Beyond all else, be patient. As they ask for answers allow them to speak but do not expect total understanding.

Be aware of body signals. Notice when they ask a question whether they look sad or confused, act out in a way that seems unrelated to what is going on around them. Ask yourself, "Does their behavior match what is going on around them?" This is a good measurement of internal turmoil. If you see the child acting in ways that do not fit the moment, step in and acknowledge their feelings.

For example, if the behavior looks angry but the moment is about ice cream, pick out the anger and focus on it. Say, "I can see that you must be mad about something" or "Looks like you feel angry. Maybe we can do something to get that anger out."

Then be creative. Assign a place to "get the anger out" or "cry the tears" or "throw the toys". Use pillows and soft toys to let the anger be expressed. In this way, the child feels safe and a part of what is going on around them. This helps them to connect those free-floating feelings to the loss of someone they knew and loved. Help them to make that connection by saying, "I really miss her/him, too, and feel like I would like to cry or throw something or get angry (whatever is appropriate for your situation with the child).

Remember, children need to release the pain of loss through grieving, healing, and hoping.

Whether it is through counseling, friends, peers, school programs, children need to have a place of hope and, healing.

They need to cultivate their memories to keep love alive and know that it is okay to do this. Sometimes they are afraid to tell a parent about this because it may seem to them that it causes the parent more pain to talk about the loss. You can help by reminding them to keep the warm smiles, tenderness, colors and textures real in their minds as well as expressing the dark, angry, side of loss. Help them to balance their feelings with the good and the bad until they can release the negative and destructive feelings and regenerate their love in the wonderful sanctuary of their memories.

Assure them about nature and the cycle of life. Let the child see a newborn baby whether child, puppy or kitten. Talk about the newness of this life and experience how fresh it is straight from God. Even a trip to the local nursery to see sprouts of trees or flowers that the child can care for will provide a great release and participation in the natural cycle of things. Planting a seed and anticipating its growth is a great way for a child to cultivate hope and anticipation for a healthy future.

By doing these simple things, a child feels as though they are part of the process of understanding, allowing them to know that life will continue. By being included, this creates an environment of feeling safe and secure. Their emotions are being validated so that they can successfully grieve. The greater the opportunity they have to participate, the better they are able to express themselves and feel loved.

"We cannot change the cards we are dealt, just how we play the hand."

Randy Pausch

Professor at Carnegie Mellon University,
author of *"The Last Lecture"*
died at 47

Husbands, Wives & Lovers

Loving and letting go

The year was 1976, and I was sitting at my graduation ceremony. Dr. Elizabeth Kubler-Ross was the commencement speaker, and the story she told was about a young woman who was recently widowed and was left with two children to raise on her own. As she spoke, I began to cry. Her words hit home, as if the speech had been selected for me alone. I too was a recent widow that had been left with my two beautiful children by my side.

There was something in that commencement speech that prompted me to change the course of my life. All those stages of denial, anger, abandonment, betrayal and acceptance were there, but in my heart I knew there was something else. I knew it was more that just losing my husband; it was about losing the cherished dream I had for my life - the dream I had held onto since I was a child. So not only did I lose the man that I loved, I lost this dream as well. And as I looked around in that commencement hall, it was then and there that I knew I had to create a new dream. I made a conscious choice to go on with a new dream, very different from the old one.

When an intimate life companion dies, the challenge is to make that love and dream into an infinite love that is eternally connected to the God-source as a step in our own evolution back to our perfect spiritual state. We must learn many lessons, dream many dreams, and seek deep within our own spirit to find the connections.

It is certainly true that we go through a lot of anger and denial in refusing to let go of our life partner. Although there is a strong and eternal bond that occurs between two people, we usually do not cultivate the spiritual aspect of it in our daily lives. We know that it is there but we do not know how to rely on it when separation occurs.

There are many things to learn about our earthly lives and spiritual transition. When someone is traveling between worlds, they are able to get in communication with our Creator. They can see beyond the periphery of physical reality, of what the mind knows, and see the grander scale of God's plan. The soul is aware of transcending this plane and returning to its whole spiritual place.

It is beautiful when two life companions can recognize the divinity of one another. The precious communication that happens between two people bound by a common dream occurs on many levels, physically, mentally, and spiritually. When you look into one another's eyes and see that spark of divinity and are really and truly cognizant of the fact that this in an individual in which God dwells, it enhances that relationship. It gives an intensity and energy that you can also depend on for healing grief and releasing your loved one.

In healing grief, you are communicating to the other person through the spiritual bond that you shared. You are telling them they are free to move on and create their perfect spiritual expression from the other side. When you can look into your heart and forgive yourself and the other person for whatever was missed, or could have been, you each begin to complete your unique and separate journeys. When you are willing to look at your emotions from the deepest level of your heart, through your soul, mind, and body, you will know without a shadow of a doubt, that it is all right to go on.

Whether or not we realize it, within our own subconscious mind we all have a dream. Part of that dream is creating, but within this physical reality, we create that dream with another person, a spouse or significant other. Two people co-join and create another energy. That energy emerges in physical communion as the powerful sexual energy that blends two people together as one, as emotional energy that mirrors our roles to each other creating the energy of a powerful drama and life story together, and spiritually in an essential energy from which all love flows into the physical and emotional. It is the spiritual energy that lets you feel the other person, know that he or she is present and influencing your life. There is this force that exists between two people that lives in their hearts. It is here that the two become one. When the other departs into pure spiritual existence, so does some of that dream.

When a life companion dies, it may seem impossible to go on. You feel the separation deep within the very cells of your body. Your emotions echo when your partner is not present to reflect them back. It is difficult to remember that the spiritual bond that you share lies beyond the conscious mind that pain and grief have filled. Anger, denial, feelings of abandonment, confusion, feeling like you have truly lost your way may overcome you. Where there is a tremendous amount of love, there is always a sense of responsibility.

It becomes difficult to remember that each

of us must make our own transition between the physical and spiritual. Each of us has a unique relationship and responsibility to the Divine. Although we have merged so completely with another person in order to learn the nature of loving and the power of sharing love, we are individual and whole unto ourselves. Completion does not come in union. Complement does.

We can never be separated from the critical communion from our Creator. No matter how glorious or tragic life may become, it is our spiritual state that allow us to touch down here for a little while to learn about loving and being loved so that we can grow in our comprehension of Divine Love.

Understanding your role in the dream that you shared often means looking at the culture and beliefs that influence us. Men, for example, may see themselves as the protectors of home and hearth. When a wife dies, men may feel so deeply flawed that they are unable to fulfill the obligations of their masculine nature. They may cut themselves off from work, children, and thoughts of the future. Feelings of pain and inadequacy make them appear aloof and indifferent. Deep inside, men feel that their flaws are so irreparable that they are unable to bond with anyone again. They may even begin to question whether the bond they shared was real since the flaw must have always been there.

Shame and guilt may cause them to withdraw. Fear may cause them to distrust their own judgment. Eventually they may secretly believe that they caused the death of their beloved. When the lies of grief infiltrate the belief system, they begin to seem real.

Women, on the other hand, often go into some expression that makes the fantasy of their own departure more real. They may seem to reject the spirit of the living and wrap themselves in fantasies of the other side while secretly wishing to die or even anticipating death. They may believe that their protector, the person that completed their existence, was their strength, the holder of their survival. They may find themselves continually going into this place.

In fact, it is the overwhelming feelings of guilt, shame, and loss of purpose that consumes their energy and clouds the mind. Feelings of anger may seem too threatening or revealing, leading to more shame. Guilt enforces secrecy and withdrawal. Feelings of abandonment rip the surviving partner from relationships with friends and family and become self-fulfilling drama.

How do we begin to dream our own dream? How do we begin to create our own new reality? How do we grieve and heal and restore the physical, emotional, and spiritual energies that seem to have left us? How is it possible for anyone to ever find healing and peace after the loss of a spouse, significant other, and lover? The immediate answer lies in invoking a state of Grace.

There is a special spiritual energy that surrounds every one of us who experiences the loss of a loved one. We must act to tap into the peace and understanding that flows directly from this God-Source. This surrounds and protects us in our weakened state of shock and bereavement. Know that this Grace is present for as long as you need it. Know that it serves to protect you. Call upon it to ease the pain so that we can shift focus into the physical.

The Divine gifts of the body must be maximized at this time of extreme stress. Fresh air, wholesome and comforting foods that nourish a system depleted through stress, movement to stimulate the metabolism, the entire physical body needs to be nourished, nurtured, and replenished.

You possess cellular memory of your life companion; your cells remember the touch, taste, smell, heat, and texture of your loved one. You need to release this so your body can heal. This is part of the withdrawal factor in losing someone you love. These are the physical consequences of losing someone that are so important to be aware of.

The spiritual level of your relationship also lives in your body in the form of networks of meridians and chakras. These networks are the energetic fields of the vital forces of each organ, physical system of the body, as well as the dynamic system of the brain and mind.

Therapies such as massage, acupuncture, acupressure, and reiki can stimulate the body's self-healing energies and restore balance to your physical functioning. Yoga, breathing exercises, stretching exercises are some very good practices that can restore a sense of health, vitality, balance. Physical therapies are essential to restoring emotional balance.

If these therapies are not available to you or you do not prefer them, substitute walking as a movement exercise. Walking will stimulate the breath, metabolism, and release the mind.

When you are beset with grief, it is difficult to see how restoring health must be an integrated process that involves the physical, mental, and spiritual. You may feel like you are on "automatic pilot" and move through the hours by constantly playing the message: "I have to go on. I have to live for (fill in the blank). I have to get this or that done for my family," rather than ask for strength during this extremely hard time.

The numbness may block out memories of the beloved that also block parts of yourself from this life. Well-meaning friends or family may even suggest that you should "put them behind you" or "try not to think about them". Healing the mind requires exactly the opposite.

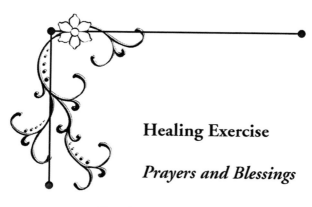

Healing Exercise

Prayers and Blessings

Go into your sacred space, and find a comfortable sitting position.

Drop your shoulders. Feel your body begin to let go of its burden as you notice a comfortable easiness move through you. Take a deep breath. Exhale. Feel the release.

Allow an image of your beloved to come into your mind. Let the image slowly come into focus.

As this image becomes clear, begin to visualize a beautiful white light forming in your chest. Feel this light move through your body, warming you, giving you peace and safety.

Watch as this beautiful white light moves from your body to your beloved. See your beloved surrounded by this white light, the light of the Divine. Hold this vision in your mind. See the peace and beauty of your beloved in this place.

When you are ready, begin to speak to your beloved. Say the words, "I wish you well. God speed. May you be free and know that my love goes with you." Know that your beloved hears your words and knows your heart. Repeat them several times, quietly as you watch each word carried on the light of the Divine to your beloved.

While you feel this connection, begin to say these words: "And may I have this Divine love and ability for myself." "God, love me." "God, be with me."

Feel the Divine light surround you and your beloved. Feel the love and freedom that each of you have to complete your journey. Feel the power of the Divine supporting you and giving you strength. Know that you are each in God's plan with a special purpose, and no love ever dies.

Allow the image to fade in your mind and notice that the strength and love stays with you. Feel a new beginning and the power of restoration stirring deep within you.

When you are ready, open your eyes and give thanks for the lessons that you have learned about love.

These simple prayers speak the power of

creation. They create the power to keep going, the power to create a new dream, and the power to remember your own unique original purpose for living this lifetime. It is your initiation that releases energy that has blocked your own senses and opens you to the eternal.

Before you leave your sacred place, speak these affirmations out loud: "I want to go on." "I will go on." "I shall go on."

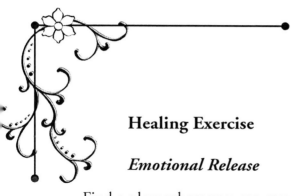

Healing Exercise

Emotional Release

Find a place where you can scream, cry, and yell. This can be a rearranging of your sacred place, or another private space where you can let some feelings out. It is important to acknowledge and release the powerful emotions that threaten the mind.

Begin this exercise by setting a time limit for your emotional release. You may want to use a timer for the exercise. The timer will tell your emotions that their time is up. You have control of them once more and they are not as powerful as you thought.

Allow your emotions to flow for a set time. If you need to throw things, prepare for the activity by buying things that you can throw that will not hurt you or your property. Some people use marshmallows, pillows, plastic items like Tupperware or other dish-type containers.

Let yourself go. Scream, yell, cry, kick, and hurl objects at the garage wall until you have exhausted the power of the emotions. Say things that you would not usually say for fear of being overheard or sounding bad. Scream at the unknown and the beyond. Let the words go without fear that they will return. Then say, "No more today," and leave this healing space.

When my husband died, I spent six hours yelling, screaming, and crying. I yelled at God, I yelled at Spirit. I wondered how I could be left alone and in this situation. I also came to understand how beneficial it was to be able to do that. This is why I share my personal experience with you, so you that you too can release some of the most difficult aspects of what you are going through.

The sacred places that you create are sanctuaries. They are the places where the energies flow physically, mentally, and spiritually. They hold and release our expressions, reflections, and healings, based on your intentions. It is where you can go and know you are completely accepted, completely loved, completely understood as a perfect God, as the parent, embraces the injured child, without judgment, without fault, in total unconditional love.

The new dream to be created is beyond the love that is shared between two people. In your sacred space, you will discover that it is not really a dream at all. It is a spiritual memory of infinite love.

Dreams, and hopes, were meant for our physical reality. We use them from day to day to move through the lessons of love. We are free in God's care to continue to dream or awaken to wholeness and understand some piece of the Divine mystery.

We are free to grow or not, free to heal or not, free to go on or not, free to receive Divine Love for the asking.

"I wanted a perfect ending. Now I've learned, the hard way, that some poems don't rhyme, and some stories don't have a clear beginning, middle, and end. Life is about not knowing, having to change, taking the moment and making the best of it, without knowing what's going to happen next. Delicious Ambiguity."

Gilda Radner

Comedienne and actress,
died at 42 of ovarian cancer

Siblings

Grieving the loss of this special relationship

When it comes to relationships, the ones we have with our siblings are like no others. We are an integral part of their lives and their reality, as they are of ours.

No matter how close in age or heart and mind, we share a special bond with our brothers and sisters. Our physical bodies share some of the same information. Our developmental experiences have similarities that do not exist in other relationships. Although we may interpret the world around us very differently, have very different points of view, talents, likes and dislikes, when it comes right down to it, our siblings are a part of us unlike any other relationship that we may have in this lifetime.

Siblings help us define who we are and what

we believe about ourselves. They help us develop our point of view in this world and are a powerful resource in our lives whether in the depth of the love we share, or through our yearnings to have a closeness that we desire. Our siblings can become our best friends, allies, or our greatest nemesis.

Whether your bond is strong with daily contact or strong in heart across distant miles, your connection to your brother or sister resonates deeply in your physical and spiritual existence. They are a reflection of our lives that only they can give. They provide a context for our family that would not exist without them. Whether they stray or return on good terms or bad, the common bond that connects siblings to each other is deep and powerful.

Sometimes people are born into a situation where sisters and brothers experience a natural estrangement because their souls have extremely different roads to walk in this lifetime. These roads can lead to estrangement and often, family problems that seem insurmountable.

I realized early that my life path was much different than that of my sister. There was one day in particular when our grandfather took us down to a newsstand and gave us each twenty-five cents. I spent my money in the blink of an eye. My sister on the other hand told my grandfather "I'm going to save my 25 cents." And she did. That moment was symbolic of things to come. Today she is vice president of a bank and her day-to-day existence is much different than mine.

My sister has never quite understood how or why I chose to spend so much time communicating with those on the other side. It was, and continues to be, outside of her scope of understanding. Perhaps that is why we do not spend as much time as we could together. She walks her path and I walk mine. Interestingly enough, it was my mother who taught me how to connect with Spirit, but she did not do the same with my sister. So I think that our lives were being driven by different influences right from the very beginning.

It was through my sister's relationship with money that she found value in living her life. It is true that on the surface we appear very different but on closer examination it becomes apparent that we are more alike than we realized, we both have spent our lives attending to the needs of others.

Many misunderstandings happen in families because we cannot comprehend that the soul and the child are sometimes at cross-purposes with each other. Sometimes we wonder, "What went wrong?" when it could simply be that the soul chose a different path before coming into the world through these parents and must follow that path at great cost so that it can learn the lessons that it needs to learn. These people are often perceived to be closer to their friends than to their family.

Other brothers and sisters may be very closely spiritually bonded in purpose and meaning. The depth of compatibility in the family may be great and the roles seemingly broader in our lives. They may seem inseparable in childhood and maintain close communication throughout their lives.

The beliefs and traditions of the family of origin may be so incorporated into their lives that there seems to be little difference between their adult households and the one they grew up in. These siblings' lives may appear to be extensions of mom and dad with the tightness of their original family unit and sibling relationships intact as adults. They may rely upon each other for resources and support, share the same values, celebrate holidays together, rear their children together in the same neighborhood where they grew up.

Whether you were very close, or separated by distance and differences, when a sibling dies, the pain of loss can feel like the loss of a deep part of yourself. You may feel as though your self-image is gone. There are always things that we wish we had said or done, times when we wish we had made a difference, and issues that never got resolved. Retrospective thoughts emerge to cause great pain when we lose someone we love, or wish we could have loved more.

Some people feel as thought their life span is affected by the death of a sibling. This is particularly the case when twin siblings experience the loss of the other. Twins grow up with a mirror of themselves that is special in the world. When twins are identical, they do, indeed, have a special bond in mind, body, and spirit that runs deeper than other children. Their commonalities blend into a single identity between them. When a twin dies, the survivor may be more affected by grief. It may be the first time in their lives that they do not have a reflection of their life experience. They may feel a sense of estrangement from the world unlike the loneliness of other survivors of sibling death.

If you are a surviving brother or sister, you may find that your beliefs about life are challenged and your identity feels uncertain. Whether you are a twin or separated by several years, the loss of a sibling is a break in the continuity of your sense of family in the world.

Sometimes the death of a sibling brings on what is called inherited guilt. If the surviving sibling inherits or receives material goods of the deceased sibling, whether it is money, clothes, or other cherished possessions, that person may feel unworthy or even that they, in some way, are collaborating with death.

If you are experiencing confusion, fear, and anxiety because of guilt and shame in addition to the pain of grief, there are some things that you can do to help you dispel those problem thoughts. The following exercise is designed to help you begin to examine your thoughts and break the hold of guilt and shame by replacing them with rational and healthy messages.

These messages will help you to transform mourning into self-nurturing so that you can redefine yourself and examine the role that your brother or sister filled in your spiritual purpose.

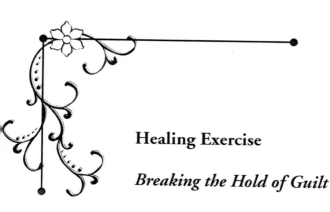

Healing Exercise

Breaking the Hold of Guilt

Create some private time for yourself. Go to your sacred space, or perhaps find a beautiful park or outdoor spot where you can spend some time writing about your feelings.

This exercise requires you to be deeply honest with yourself about your thoughts and feelings. Do not fear that you are crazy or feel embarrassed about the thoughts that you have. What you are writing is private, for your eyes only.

Use plain paper for this exercise, rather than writing in your healing journal, so that you can perform a healing ritual at the end of the task.

Sit comfortably and quietly. Try to find a place where you will not be distracted. Take a deep breath and exhale by blowing out. Take a second deep breath and blow out with force. This will help you to gather courage and clarity.

Begin by listening to the chatter in your head. Let the thoughts form and come into your mind. Look at the thoughts that have been making you feel guilty or ashamed.

Some thoughts may be of competition between you and your deceased sibling. Some may be of you having or getting "more out of life" than the other. You may discover thoughts that compare the two of you. Memories of things that you did or did not do that you believe had some impact on the life of your sibling and causes you regret.

Allow these thoughts to emerge and begin to write them down. Number them: 1., 2., 3.

When you have finished writing five thoughts, turn to a new page in your journal or use another piece of paper. Begin to write the following statements:

1. Death is not the result of competition. No one wins and no one loses. It is a natural event in the cycle of God's plan.

2. Death is not the result of an exchange of words or an omission of words in things said or unsaid.

3. Death has no scoreboard.

4. Bad thoughts do not cause death.

5. Whatever inheritance I receive, whether small or large, memories or material goods, does not constitute collaborating with death. I cannot know God's plan.

When you have finished take the page of negative thoughts set fire to it. Be sure that you hold the paper over the kitchen sink or a sandy spot or a barbeque grill where there is no possibility of getting burned or setting fire to other objects.

As the paper turns to ash, visualize the painful thoughts going up in smoke.

Keep your page of rational thoughts that now replace those in your mind. Read them whenever you feel the pull of distorted or self-punishing thoughts to keep a clear and positive mind to heal your grief.

Return to your sacred place and say a simple prayer of thanks. Allow feelings of gratitude to emerge while you are in your sacred place. Feel the beauty of God's love enter your mind after you have cleared away the distortions.

You may repeat this exercise as often as necessary to help change your perspective.

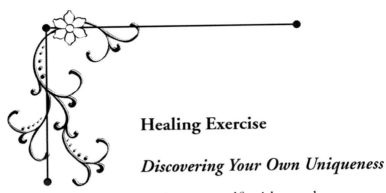

Healing Exercise

Discovering Your Own Uniqueness

Rediscovering yourself without the context of your sibling is the transformational task that lies before you. Each of us moves through this life on our own path. It is easy to forget that all of us are uniquely on our own in this life. We are here to learn the lessons about love that we chose from the spirit realm.

In the Divine plan, we are all interdependent, and are given many beautiful as well as painful relationships from which to learn. Often we put off learning, and the deep examination of our purpose, until death gets our attention.

Healing grief is possible and necessary if you are to see the deeper meaning of who and what you are, and discover your connection to the ever-flowing Divine Love that sustains you.

Begin this healing process by examining the role of your brother or sister in your life. Ask yourself these questions:

"What kind of sibling am I?"

"What was my contribution to this relationship?"

"What lessons have I learned about being a sibling?"

"What kind of love do I know about?"

"What can I take forth from these lessons?"

"How has being a sibling formed the direction of my life?"

"What choices have I made because I am a sibling that may have been different had I been an only child?"

"What is uniquely mine in the sibling relationship?"

"How do I express my uniqueness in the world?"

"What was unique to my sibling, and how did that uniqueness affect me?"

"What do I want to preserve and take forth into my life?"

Be patient with yourself. This exercise is not finished in an hour or a day. Use it repeatedly as your mind begins to open to healthy thoughts and new energies. Use your journal to write your thoughts as they come into your mind.

Focus on the love that flows between you and your sibling and know that you are connected to Divine Love that makes all love and healing possible.

Our Beloved Pets

As a teenager, I was a pudgy kid. As you know, kids can be cruel. They made fun of me and my weight, and it always brought me to tears. It was the small Dachshund Dixie Bell that overheard my sorrows and kissed (rather licked) the tears away. Such divine love and compassion was in this little dog, who in her own way healed the hurt of a teenage girl. How can we ever forget these pets that we love so dearly?

How many times have we sat down with a pet and talked about the day, or why this or that went wrong, or even about our good times during the day? We treasure those moments when we cried and felt that cold nose, soft paw, or smooth feathers that said to us, "You are not alone. I am here." Our companion animals have a remarkable sensitivity and awareness of our feelings that needs no explanation. It is a gift from the Divine to those who have a heart that can open to sharing the life experience with some of God's beautiful creatures.

Anyone who has ever had a relationship with a pet, or welcomed a companion animal into their life knows the tenderness, the vulnerability, the strength, and bond that are formed between us. There are moments that we share with other animals that we would not share with humans because we know that our beloved pets will not judge or reject us for our shortcomings. When no one else in the world seems to understand, love, and abide with you, the cherished animal companion is there to assure us that we are loved, and never alone.

In some great and mysterious way our pets are able to share our deepest moments. It is that special experience of unconditional love that feels so close in purity to our spiritual memories of the perfect love from that realm.

We are driven by the desire to love and be loved. Pets show us how to give and receive. Just as there are people who find wounded animals to heal, there are wounded people who are healed by these animals. For example, when there is a death in the family, a pet seems to understand the grief and instinctively offers consolation in the form of silent, loving observation and diligence. Their very breath, life, vitality is deeply connected to yours.

Their eyes look into ours and acknowledge that we are not alone. Their spontaneity forces us to move in concert with them in a rhythm that can bring us back to life.

A friend once told me that it was impossible to feel sad while looking at a penguin. I thought about their funny shape and waddling walk and laughed out loud. God loves all his creatures and connects us in ways that we have yet to discover.

Healing our minds and bodies and restoring our soul is one of their greatest contributions to the life that we share.

Animals pierce through the weight of our feelings and draw us into health. For example, it is also impossible to feel sad while holding a puppy. Their newness and energy seem to come straight from the God-Source into our lives with an enthusiasm and trust that is undeniable for even the hardest of hearts. Their love and trust flows freely and can fill a room that would otherwise seem empty with fifty people in it.

Some of us have very fond memories from childhood of special pets that shared our secrets when mom or dad could not. Without word or deed, excuses or explanations, the love that exists between pets and people is deeply intimate and profoundly significant. They bring us hope, unity, and compassion that go beyond words.

Imagine the little turtle or hamster that hears a child's prayers, or listens when they talk about life. How many pets save lives by rescuing people or alerting us to danger. How many raise our children and hear the secrets that parents will never know? It is never "just a dog", or "only a fish."

Animals are our special companions, here for reasons that we may never fully understand but there is one thing that we can know for certain, and that is, God loves them, created them, and will call to them from his eternal place to return. No matter what the circumstances of your pet's death, they, too, make the transition back into their perfect spiritual state.

We have all kinds of relationships with animals. Medical research has proven that having a relationship with a pet promotes health and well-being. Animal therapy is a wonderful treatment that is welcomed by many hospitals, convalescent and rehabilitation centers, mental health practitioners, and developmental centers as an adjunct treatment for various disabilities. It is well documented that just holding a dog or a cat can help with stress, blood pressure, grief, motivation, and even the will to live. The presence of pets has been known to reduce recovery time from surgery and enhance the quality of life for those with chronic illnesses. Many studies have tested the psychic abilities of dogs and their uncanny ability to know when their people are in trouble, sick, or distressed.

Whether snake, hamster, fish, bird, rabbit, cat, dog, or turtle, our pets are a part of our journey through this life and have a special role in our lessons about love. Across all the peaks and valleys of our lives our pets help us to heal and give us a glimpse of our own soul.

There is no doubt, when a beloved animal dies we can be devastated by the loss. If you are suffering the loss of a precious companion animal, you have been given a very special gift from the Divine. It is a privilege to share a part of your life with God's beloved creatures. And it is their final gift to us that they teach us about impermanence, the ability to love and then having to let go. These loving animals give us the insight, understanding and wisdom that we can love and let go. They can be one of the first loves of our life that teach us about impermanence and timeless love.

Even in their absence, you can sense the cold wet nose, the nuzzling, the smell of their fur or habitat for months, sometimes even years, after their departure back to the God-Source.

Allow yourself to grieve, and seek the company of those people who understand and acknowledge the bond you shared.

As you heal from grief over this loss, you will learn something very important about your spirit and the bond with your pet. Of course they teach us how to grow and be responsible, but, they also show us our soul and a little about this life and the next.

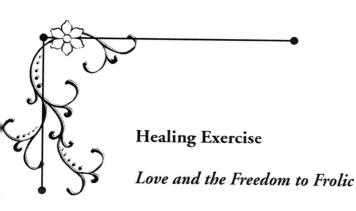

Healing Exercise

Love and the Freedom to Frolic

Healing the loss of a cherished pet occurs in the deep inner silence, the same space that you shared in communion.

Go into your sacred space and create silence that will transport you back into that deep special place inside where you and your cherished pet shared those special moments.

Breathe deeply. Close your eyes and invite a beautiful memory of your pet to come into your awareness.

Feel the warmth in your heart, the unity, the unconditional love and companionship.

Begin to visualize a white light in your body. Move this white light to surround your pet, send the light, feel it leaving your body and moving to your pet. Then visualize the light moving from the pet's heart center back to yours, filling you with warmth, and flooding you with unconditional love.

Send the love back to the pet and feel that love growing larger and larger until it expands into the universe.

Release the love and know that it is always there. At any time, you can return and share these moments of spiritual intimacy with the animal whose journey through this life met with yours for a short while.

Thank them for what they have given you.

Tell them that they fulfilled their purpose.

Release them with God-speed and the freedom to guide your spirit in that realm.

See them moving on to some of their own happiest places, whether this is a pet running in an open field or swimming in a giant aquarium, visualize them as being happy.

Feel their peaceful, joyful bounding through eternity and know that your bond transcends words and physical boundaries.

Allow yourself to shed tears and turn those

tears of sadness to tears of joy that they are whole and perfect.

Slowly open your eyes and return to the objects in your sacred place. Feel the gratitude for their devotion fill your heart and know that you can return at anytime for a glimpse of this spiritual connection.

*"For certain is death for the born
And certain is birth for the dead;
Therefore over the inevitable
Thou shouldst not grieve."*

Bhagavad Gita - Chapter 2

Suicide & Forgiveness

Suicide is an expression of not being able to cope with life.

I've consoled many clients who are not able to comprehend why their beloved left in such a manner. Once again, we are reminded that we each experience this life in different ways and handle things very differently. When someone is thinking about committing suicide, it is because they can not see any earthly solution to their problems.

Years ago, one of my clients, the mother of a teenage boy, wept on my couch for hours because her son had recently taken his own life. He could not cope with pressures of high school, and to mask his pain he got into drugs which affected his perceptions and put him on an emotional roller coaster. In his mind, the only way to end the pain was to end his life. His mother was able to find a sense of peace that he was alright and the love that she shared with this child would go on.

There is a myth in our society that perfection is attainable in this life and that it is necessary for success, health, and happiness. Our lives are filled with media messages, from radio, television, movies, and the bigger-than-life entertainment, that perfection has value and all else is worthless.

When we look at the person who is "the model of success" these messages infiltrate our personal belief systems. We equate success with perfection, beauty with perfection, acceptance with perfection and being loveable with perfection. These messages have worked their way into our belief systems since childhood. From the critical voice inside our heads we hear: Perfection equals success in health, wealth, and relationships and personal value.

The huge expenditure of energy that is wasted on striving to be perfect and criticizing those who are not is often the cause of loss of love, friendship, and our true place in the world because the guilt and self-loathing that results from our unrelenting comparisons to models of perfection leaves us constantly focused on our flaws. Some of us try to hide them. Others try to "work on them" like they should be replaced with better parts from the store, or at least cosmetically covered up if not surgically changed. Our guilt about not being free to be who and what we really are leads us into self-punishment and rejection that cripples our ability to love and believe ourselves to be lovable. How can you believe that the Divine loves you if you believe that you are not worth loving?

Nearly every day I hear something about the perfect family, the perfect mate, the perfect job, the perfect house, the perfect retirement plan, and on and on. But life is not lived in perfection. Perfection is not the norm. Our perceptions are like dreams from which we must awaken and learn about love.

With our deeply engrained beliefs about perfection, an untimely death presents us with the cold reality of the breach between this life and the next. Sadly, it is not until we are confronted with the unnaturalness of suicide that our eyes are opened to the preciousness of our life cycle and our misdirected concerns about our daily lives.

Our friends serve a very special purpose in our lives. People become friends through a variety of circumstances. Some friendships develop because of time spent together at work, school, during special projects or neighborhood interests. Through numerous opportunities, we meet and develop friendships with people that serve a very important role in our lives, no matter how casual. You can have a friend that you have not seen in years that is just as precious to you as though you spend time talking every day. Others may share your time everyday and are taken for granted until their absence creates a void in our lives.

We need people to live, to grow, to help us through our daily struggles and to celebrate our triumphs. At the spiritual level, the people that we meet are never coincidental. They serve a very important role in our lives that originates with our spiritual origins.

When someone we know takes matters into their own hands and ends their life, it has a profound impact on us, no matter how intimate or seemingly distant the relationship.

In coping with the loss of someone from suicide, it is helpful to take a look at the kind of intimacy you shared. One way to do this, rather than just think about memories, is to participate in a simple exercise that will let you get a better grasp on how that person touched your life.

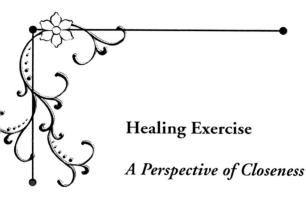

Healing Exercise

A Perspective of Closeness

On a plain piece of paper, draw five circles, each one within the other. Place a dot in the center of the inner circle.

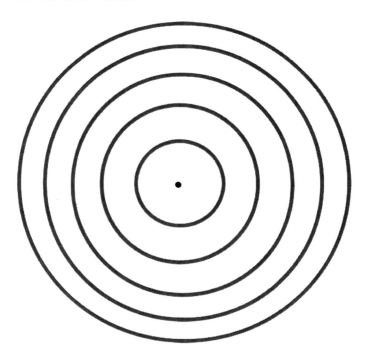

Begin to ask yourself some questions about the role of this person in your life:

> "Did we share tears of happiness or sadness about something?"

> "Did I depend on this person for something?"

> "Is there something that I wanted to say or ask and never did?"

> "Did I put off doing something that I intended to do?"

> "Did we share differing points of view on issues at work, play, or as neighbors?"

> "Is the person a friend of a friend, or were they close to someone that is close to me but really unknown to me?"

As you think about these questions, begin to see where this person would fit in the circles.

A best friend, good friend at work, good friend of the family may fit in the inner circle with you. Sometimes a peer, although you may not have seen someone since school days, can be dearly missed because you shared a part of your lives at an earlier time but grew apart in adulthood. These people may also fit in the inner circle with you.

Place a dot in the circle that best represents the closeness of the person to you. This can help you begin to understand the depth of feelings that you may be experiencing due to the suicide of a person in your life.

Because of the powerful impact that suicide has in the natural life-giving order of things, we should not underestimate its impact on our lives. Grief, no matter how seemingly brief makes its mark on all of us. It is to be respected, worked through, and used as an opportunity to grow in love and understanding of a little more of God's plan. When suicide touches our lives we are most abruptly and violently reminded that we cannot know another's destiny or purpose in God's plan.

No matter what the circumstances, or how close we are to the deceased it is extremely difficult to resolve our thoughts and feelings about the act of taking life and death into our own hands in suicide.

Our spiritual purpose is to be in alignment and continually connected with God. From the spiritual perspective, the suicidal impulse comes from a misalignment deep within the soul from its original purpose. This misalignment causes total angst about this lifetime that results in constant internal torment that most of us cannot imagine. It is as though the person cannot find the connection between the spirit and his or her place in this life cycle - this lifetime, yet, there seems to exist the deeper sense that there is a connection. They observe that others have a balance and alignment that integrates body, mind, and soul, but for them it seems impossible.

The risk that they take of walking into the unknown while reaching for peace can only originate with some spiritual memory that calls to them like a homing device. We are all equipped with that homing device as our failsafe. But to see it activated in suicide is devastating to the natural order of life. We cannot know God's plan. We cannot know the inevitability of that life.

Whether the suicide emerged from mental illness, trauma, fear, or chronic problems, or happened suddenly and "out of the blue", we are only left with a deep sense that our innocence has been violated and we feel guilty, helpless and chaotic. We worry about the spirit of the deceased and our own responsibility in such an act.

Even therapists require professional support when a patient decides to leave this world by taking his or her own life. Some leave the profession because of the overwhelming pain and sense of responsibility and helplessness.

Ultimately, the only way that we can accept and reconcile the impact of losing someone through suicide is to understand that it is between him or her and God. God's Divine plan has a deeper order than we are capable of comprehending.

Traditional religious views

It is true that some traditional religions condemn the act of suicide, and consign these individuals to hell. I believe that the hell is within people's minds. Know that the Divine never leaves us - not any one of us, even in suicide. The soul and spirit is completely in God's hands. There is no punishment or forsaken state to fear, for God loves all his creation and will guide each spirit safely home.

Under these terrible circumstances, we are cruelly reminded that our preoccupation with perfection is destructive. Love and acceptance is what we must strive for under all conditions and in all circumstances. Our purpose for this lifetime is to love and be loved through tolerance, acceptance, patience, and service. To be a part of goodness, to have worth and manifest that worth in this world gives meaning to our lives.

It is our imperfections that teach us to love, to be accepting of others, to look beyond the surface into the depth of what we really are. Our flaws give us meaning, motivation, and unique identity. Just as in nature, imperfection is considered beautiful; the imperfections of our own nature give us beauty. It is through our imperfections that each of us adds something unique to the world.

We can be a facilitator for someone else, but we cannot know his or her destiny. We are sometimes called to intercede in someone else's life, but we are not responsible for their choices. With these thoughts in mind, the following meditation is designed to help with the guilt and shame that happens when someone we know takes his or her own life.

Healing Exercise

Forgiveness & Godspeed

This exercise can be done daily if the intensity of your feelings, or continual thoughts of the incident, are interfering with your daily life. It is important for you to release your feelings and use your thoughts to send positive assistance to this spirit in very special need during this time of transition.

Return to your sacred space and light a candle to symbolize the light of forgiveness and the light of the Spirit that guides your prayers.

Begin to count backwards from ten to one. Close your eyes and let the numbers come into your mind by themselves. Relaxing: Ten . . . Nine . . Eight. . . Seven ... Six ... Five . . . Four . . . Three . . . Two . . . One ...

When you reach the number one begin to visualize a ball of white light forming in your center. See it grow.

Feel the healing warmth of the white light begin to move through your body. See the light move outside of you and surround you, protecting you.

Begin to float on the light as if you were floating on the beautiful glow that surrounds you.

Breathe a deep breath in with the silent count of five. Feel the energy from the light fill your lungs as you hold with a count of three before you exhale, very slowly. Relax, float on the light as it moves in and around you. Breathe in again inhaling for a silent count of five. Feel the light growing stronger, more beautiful, more warm and comforting. Exhale very slowly to a silent count of three.

For the third time, take a deep breath of the light that surrounds you and fills your lungs. Feel it vitalize your body. Exhale slowly.

With the healing light surrounding you, protecting you, healing you from the inside out, repeat the following prayer:

Oh Heavenly Being of Light,
allow the release of my loved one.

I know that their transition was within the Divine
Order, and that their soul decided it was time for
them to be with you anew.

Help me, Almighty One, to release the pain, to
release the sorrow and to let them go.

Let me know in my heart and soul
that it was time for them to be free.

Let me know in my heart and mind
that it is time for me to let them go.

I know there is a Greater Plan.
Let me feel your peace.

Let me be an instrument of that peace, so that I can
send light and love to this beloved soul
whose struggle is now over.

May I be able to find the courage and the strength
to release my own confusion, my own pain, my own
hurt, and my own lack of understanding.

*Allow me the strength to create a new reality where
I can find wisdom, where I can be at peace with the
fact that this loved one
is no longer with us in the physical body.*

*Allow me to rest in peace as my loved one journeys
forward to further freedom
and to create a different awareness.*

*I thank you, and I know that
this peace is already within me.*

I Love You, Goodbye

The healing process goes on

Even though this book is coming to an end, your healing journey is an ongoing process.

There will be times when the healing process seems to progress slowly, other times sudden spontaneous healing fills you with joy and energy. I encourage you to be patient and persistent. Be gentle with yourself. Let hope be your guide and know that Divine Love is always available to you.

Most of us spend a great deal of time trying to sort things out in a logical way as a means of coping with the loss of a loved one. Unfortunately, death is not logical. As we struggle to bring some closure we often question our preparedness, efforts, and responsibilities, but there was never enough time for all of the things we loved to do or intended to do for our beloved.

Death, and the finality of our physical existence, makes a tremendous impact on all our lives. It reminds us of our inability to reverse circumstances, imposes sudden and permanent change that throws our lives into chaos, and exacts a terrible toll in grief.

However, healing grief and working through the losses can be one of our most meaningful growth processes. The death event presents us with a time of peak awareness wherein, if we allow ourselves, we can learn more about who and what we are. It is a process that takes great courage.

Understand that fear of the unknown, shame, and how we each view our personal inadequacies manifest throughout all our lives. Success is in how we interpret them, overcome them, and use them to gain a deeper understanding of love, acceptance, and forgiveness.

You can heal grief. You can overcome loss and renew your hopes and dreams through deepening your understanding of the special roles that each person in your life has fulfilled.

It takes courage to forgive, and it takes courage to live life to the fullest. It also takes unleashed creativity. Your vitality is in the creative process. It is the place of dreams, the home of your true identity, and the energy of healing through the Divine. God creates and endows each one of us with the power to renew ourselves all throughout this earthly journey. Grief is a catalyst to renewal in our physical and spiritual existence. Trust in God and in your Divine endowment that there is an unbroken communication within the heart, mind, and spirit.

We cannot change our state within until we are willing to let go of hatred, shame, regret, and anger. These negative emotions imprison us and will certainly bring on illness. These emotions block healing energies and keep us from spiritual wisdom.

It is a time for action rather than intention. The healing process is an active and dynamic experience through the work of your healing journey.

Return to the meditations and exercises in this book and use them often. Let the prayers and affirmations carry you through the difficult moments until calmness and order are restored in your life.

Healing Exercise

Maintaining Perspective

The following is an exercise that I use to help maintain my perspective about what is really important in life. It helps to keep me focused when the daily business of living seems to steal time away from loving activities.

The exercise is simple. If you had three months to live your life in any way that you chose, and knew that you were going to die quietly and without pain at the end of three months, how would you live your life?

What would you do?

Would you spend it hating?

Seeking retribution?

Feeling sorry for yourself?

Celebrating in blissful joy?

Bringing peace and happiness to those you love?

Giving of the very best that you are to those in need?

What would you do for your loved ones?

What would you have them do for you?

How would you change your relationship to each person in your life?

How would you change your relationship to your Creator?

How would you prepare to let go and leave this life?

Letting go is the ultimate act of trust and faith. Trust in yourself. Know that you can find the source of Divine Love within you and say: "I love you, goodbye, and God-speed."

Classes and Consultations with Dr. Bell

Patricia Bell teaches classes on a variety of topics including healing grief, astrology, and mediumship in locations around the world. She has been teaching at the Learning Annex for several years. Below are a few examples of what students at the Learning Annex think about Patricia's classes.

Student Feedback:

• A very engaging speaker, a perfect balance of her life story & experience, the process of mediumship and afterlife and "greetings" for individuals at the seminar.

• Wonderful....Patricia Bell is gifted and a great teacher.

• Patricia was so SO good! She was phenomenal!

• Very much enjoyed....very informative and healing!!!

• Patricia Bell was outstanding! She captured the emotions of everyone in the audience. Her approach to meditating was thoughtful and unique. She had everyone's attention for the full class. I could have sat there for another hour because I thought she was so insightful and compassionate at the same time. She really is an angel!

• Dr. Bell blew me away ... her knowledge of spirituality was incredible. She held my attention throughout the entire evening. I was sorry when it was over. Bravo ... please bring her back!!! Often!!!!

• I have been to a fair number of psychics, and this was one of the best!

• This was a wonderful experience and I would recommend it...I went into to this with no preconceived concepts and have come away with a feeling of peace, along with an appreciation and admiration for Patricia Bell and her work.

• This was THE BEST seminar I have ever been to from you guys... HANDS DOWN!!!

To contact Dr. Bell, learn more about upcoming classes, or for a personal consulation visit:

www.PatriciaBell.net

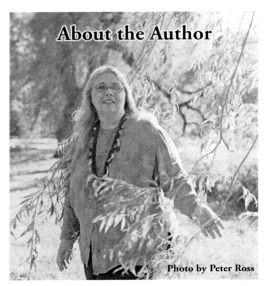

About the Author

Photo by Peter Ross

Dr. Patricia Bell's unique talents as a Spiritualist minister, medium, author, lecturer, and healer have helped people through the grieving process for the past 35 years. She travels throughout the world sharing the message that life goes on after death.

Dr. Bell graduated from the University of Miami and the International College of Spiritual Sciences in Montreal with a Ph.D. in Humanities.

Although she takes great pride in her work, one of her favorite jobs is being Grandmother to Bailey and Alexandria.

To learn more about Dr. Bell visit:
www.PatriciaBell.net

Breinigsville, PA USA
07 May 2010
237524BV00005B/1/P